So You're Seventy ... So What?

How to Love the Years You Thought You'd Hate

Also by Maralys Wills

The Tail on my Mother's Kite

Buy a Trumpet and Blow Your Own Horn:
Turning Books into Bucks

Damn the Rejections, Full Speed Ahead:
The Bumpy Road to Getting Published

A Clown in the Trunk: A Memoir

A Circus Without Elephants: A Memoir

Save My Son

Scatterpath: A Thriller

Higher Than Eagles: The Tragedy and Triumph
of an American Family

Fun Games for Great Parties

Soar and Surrender

A Match for Always

Mountain Spell

Tempest and Tenderness

Man Birds: Hang Gliders & Hang Gliding

So You're Seventy ... So What?

How to Love the Years You Thought You'd Hate

MARALYS WILLS

LEMON LANE PRESS • SANTA ANA, CALIFORNIA

Praise for *So You're Seventy ... So What?*

Well, Maralys, you've really done it this time. Your audience is going to relate personally to each and every chapter. Your humor is smack on.

JAN MURRA, AUTHOR *Cast Off*

You will find this delightful, engaging, helpful, and beautifully-written book impossible to put down. From learning about Posit Science to enhance your brain, to opening a bag of peanuts, to the miracles of vitamin C, this book may change your life and help you enjoy it to the fullest.

DOROTHY NELSON, J.D.

Maralys Wills' book is filled with candid, real-life examples that kept me reading—and in places laughing out loud. But more important, it contains practical information presented in an easy-to-read style—tips that will help make your good years even better

IRENE BERARDESCO, B.A.

It sounds too good to be true. The title of Maralys' latest book makes one wonder: How can we really love those "Golden Years" just ahead—or already upon us? Mixing practical hints with her usual humor,

Maralys gives us an enjoyable read, plus common sense strategies for dealing with the inevitable. As is her style, she draws from her own experiences, offering readers clever ways to cope.

LINDA MAYEDA, M.A.

Maralys Wills is a great date and a cheap doctor. By happy chance, I had been reading her practical, entertaining book on the very day I tried to put on panty hose for the first time in ten years. During my slow-motion fall to the bathroom floor, I realized a couple of things: a) I really don't need to wear panty-hose again; I haven't worn a dress in decades. 2) Maralys has an antidote—and anecdote—for every accident I've had in the last two years. And that's saying a lot.

STEPHANIE EDWARDS,
EMMY-WINNING MEDIA COMMENTATOR,
AUTHOR OF, *I Won't be Back After These Messages*

Fresh and funny if you're under 70. Familiar and comforting if you've been there, Maralys Wills' new book is her You Tube memories, the literary gems of her fabulous life.

THEA CLARK, PhD
AUTHOR, *No! Your Other Left Foot*

*Dedicated to
Hillary Clinton, Sandra
Day O'Conner, and Dorothy
Nelson, three amazing women
whose achievements have
been an inspiration to women
everywhere.*

Contents

ACKNOWLEDGEMENTS

My first, most important thanks go to my husband, Rob. More than ever he supported me by bringing in meals, making sure I had enough time to work, listening to chapters as I finished them, offering insightful comments.

Additional thanks go to my critique group: Barbara French, Pam Tallman, Allene Symons, P.J. Penman, Terry Black, and Erv Tibbs. As always, the group has been there for me, picking up the spirit of what I'm doing and offering ways to make chapters clearer and livelier. When I needed extra help, one or another would pitch in without hesitation.

Thanks go to Wellprint, Inc. in Tustin: to Don, Jim, and Heather, who offered all the publishing help an author could ask for.

And a final thanks for the readers who added their enthusiasm and comments to my project: Dorothy Nelson, Linda Mayeda, Irene Berardesco, Jevelyn Margines, and Jan Murra.

Chapter One

Introduction

I once knew the definition of "old." It was anyone twenty years older than I was.

At age forty-nine, my friends and I made a lot of arrogant snap judgments, imagining we knew over-the-hill when we saw it … you know, the snow-capped head, the forward-tilted posture, the scurrying out for dinner at four in the afternoon.

Who knew how fast those twenty years would melt away—or how anything-but-old most of us would then feel?

Now that my husband and I sometimes head out for dinner at 4:15 (because how else will I make the class I teach at 6:30?) or occasionally, like Seinfeld's parents, because we're simply hell bent on making Soup Plantation's Early Bird special … now that I haven't seen my real hair color in this century … it's time to declare that "old" must mean some other age. And someone else. Surely it doesn't apply to me.

And if it doesn't, why not?

Herein I offer the little bag of tricks that can make Seventy seem even younger than middle-aged … or anyway, younger than you once believed.

P.S. You'll notice that this book, while not succumbing to a call for larger type, is largely autobiographical. As with my writing books, it's easiest to teach from experiences I've actually lived through—from the various situations I know first-hand.

Chapter Two

Balance and Tripping

This may seem wild, crazy, and a big fat lie, but for many of us the years from seventy to eighty are one of the best decades of our lives.

We don't catch many colds (our immune systems have already met most of the available bugs), we don't seem to need much food (and younger relatives keep inviting us to dinner), we've learned not to take off-handed comments personally, and senior discounts seem to pop up everywhere.

But there's more. If we're still married, we've figured out that marital fights are mostly a waste of energy. Even brief separations can make us wives feel like teenagers, ridiculously thrilled to see that wonderful old guy once again. Hey, who's the handsome, gray-haired fellow in the chair, looking up with a grin as you come in the door?

Appreciation for each other becomes a palpable ingredient in a long marriage.

As long as you feel good, what's not to like about seventy?

As a normal part of every age, though, keeping a grip on happiness takes effort. For instance, there's the issue of balance and tripping.

Unless you're watching an astronaut preparing for the moon, there are better things to think about than what becomes of a body flying through space.

That is, until the body is yours.

For some of us, catching a toe on the ottoman and sailing away like a stretched rubber band, is an everyday possibility.

One of my very dear friends was plagued, in her late seventies, by frequent falls. Each one was a physical set back ... and some later became calamities.

Though Barbara was a gifted artist and a mental giant—as sharp as any college professor—her body betrayed her and she kept stumbling over normal, everyday objects, like garden furniture and sidewalk curbs.

None of those falls did her any good, and some were followed by trips to the hospital, where a few days in bed only made her legs more wobbly.

Frankly, I'd never thought much about balance—mostly because it had never been a problem. Until something bugs you, why worry about fixing it?

And then one day I had the craziest accident.

I'd gone out the front door to retrieve some theater tickets off the porch. Bending over has never been a challenge. But as I started to straighten, the inexplicable happened. I couldn't get my feet under me.

Whether it was my new, extra-fat tennis shoes or a simple loss of balance, I'll never know. I was only aware that I found myself lurching, pedaling, flailing, slap-stepping in my bloated tennis shoes, trying to regain my feet. And somehow not managing to do it.

Instead, all that fancy foot work launched me off the porch and out over our two front steps. Literally out into space.

I was airborne long enough to realize there was no soft landing in sight, that cement was everywhere and I would inevitably hit our inlaid-stone walkway. Horrified as I sailed, I came down from an exaggerated altitude and smacked hard onto the stones.

For seconds I lay sprawled, unable to move. It hurt to breathe. But I was alive. I was conscious. And I hadn't hit my head.

I could see my right wrist was torn up, and God knows what else.

From my ungainly splat on the walkway, I yelled through the still-open front door, trying to attract my husband.

He didn't seem to hear. Which was nothing new.

Struggling to sit up, I could see him across the

family room, calmly watching television.

"Rob!" I screamed. "Rob! Help!"

He paid no attention, seemed riveted to the TV.

"Rob!" I screamed even louder, "Rob! Rob! Rob! Help!"

Some part of me wondered how, for an injured person, I'd managed to yell so loud.

At last he stirred, as though awakening from a dream.

"Babe?" He leaned forward. "What's going on?"

"Help me!"

"What?" He pulled himself to his feet, ambled out to the porch. "What happened? What are you doing down there?"

Taking a nap. "I fell." A shallow, painful breath. "Off the porch." Another breath. "I've been yelling."

"Jesus, that was you? I thought it was the television. They were showing the Challenger coming apart. People were screaming on TV."

He now stood over me, baffled. "I finally realized it wasn't all television—it was you. Where are you hurt?"

"I don't know. Everywhere."

He reached down a hand. "Can you get up? If I help?"

"No."

"I'm not sure I can lift you, Babe. You'd be a dead weight." He thought a moment. "I'll call Chris. Maybe he's home." He looked down at me again. "Good God, look at your wrist."

"I know. It's a mess. I'm probably a mess in other places."

"I'll go call."

Chris was our son, an orthopedic surgeon who lived half a mile away. Rob disappeared and was back in minutes.

"He just got home, Babe. He'll be right down."

I nodded, instantly relieved. I was alive. And Chris was coming. For the moment nothing else mattered.

CHRIS IS ONE OF THOSE DOCTORS WHO MAKES YOU feel better simply by showing up. That goes for his wife, too.

They arrived together, Betty-Jo with a warm look of sympathy, Chris with his usual aura of concern, almost a smile. The smile, or near smile, is reserved for non-emergencies. I was breathing, talking, clearly not a life or death case.

Chris looked me over, felt my ribs.

"Ouch! Ouch!"

"May be broken. We have to get you up." He turned to his dad. "Still got that walker—the one with a seat?"

Rob said he did, and minutes later, Betty-Jo, Chris, and Rob eased me up onto the seat and pulled me up the two steps and into the family room. I explained what had happened.

With a gentle touch, Chris once more probed and prodded my ribs. "Well, Mom," he said cheerfully, "they're probably broken, but even if they are, it won't make any difference. We don't do anything. Just let them heal on their own." He grinned. "Don't try to lift any pianos."

"I'll make it a point."

"For awhile it'll hurt to breathe. Take a few painkillers." He examined my torn-up wrist. "Here, we'll clean this. Anyplace else?"

I pointed to my well-scraped ankle.

"Okay. We'll take care of that too. You got off lucky, you know. All your other bones are intact. From now on you might also try to avoid the front porch."

THE REPERCUSSIONS WENT ON FOR A FEW WEEKS. X-rays showed I was even luckier than Chris imagined: no ribs were cracked. But then my son has often remarked on our family's inherited sturdiness. "You and I, Mom, have the bones of a dinosaur. Hopefully we've got a better future."

The second thing I did was send back those extra-fat tennis shoes.

Eventually Chris suggested that Rob and I go to rehab for balance training. For a month the two of us played balance games: Walked on uneven surfaces.

Threw a ball back and forth as we strolled. Balanced on one leg. Strengthened our legs on a resistance bicycle.

It all helped. But then our allotted Medicare visits termed out. So I tackled the balance issue another way.

On my own, each day I stood near a table I could grab onto and practiced standing one-legged, first on one side, then the other, always for a count of 50.

Eventually this quick-and-easy trick paid off. I seemed to recover from momentary stumbles. To my astonishment, I was finally able to put on my trousers any old place, any old time, without sitting down.

I doubt that putting-on-one's-pants will ever qualify as an Olympic event ... meaning there's no gold medal in my future. But hey, I'm now dressing the way I did at age forty. If that isn't some kind of victory, I don't know what is.

For seventy-plusers the balance issue is huge. But then so is the matter of tripping.

A few years ago I learned a painful lesson about leaving big things in bad places—like the mid-day when I dropped off a box of books in the service porch, and how I came home after dark and didn't see it, and did a half-gainer right into our extra freezer. Luckily, it wasn't open.

There's a rule in our house: never leave *anything* in your normal pathways. Push everything off to the sides, to places where you don't walk.

A temporary solution for stuff you should put away—but organized clutter is better than an unexpected journey to the emergency room.

There's a mantra going here: *anything* you can do to stay on your feet, to remain upright by choice is definitely worth the effort.

CHAPTER THREE

Your Brain and ... What Was That Other Thing?

IN OUR HOUSE THERE'S A LOT OF ONGOING COMPE-
tition, which I freely admit to friends, but as one of them
says with a laugh, "It's rivalry just short of warfare."

For no particular reason, Rob and I keep measuring
each other, comparing what we do with what the other
one does, as though there's some Otherbeing out there
keeping track—as though it's Rob's duty to keep that
Otherbeing informed.

"You cheated on the Crossword, Babe. I gave you
one of the answers, so it doesn't count."

"Doesn't count for what?"

"You can't claim you did it."

"Do you see me claiming anywhere? Besides, you
only helped with one clue."

"Well, don't say you finished, because you didn't."

I stare at him and shrug. *Who would I say it to?* We
go on like that, both of us vying for the catbird seat.
Who plays the better game of Sequence, who saves the

most gas when he drives, who spends the fewest minutes looking for misplaced papers, who has the better memory.

Privately, I concede that Rob wins on memory. Except when he doesn't. For a man who manages to outscore half the contestants on *Jeopardy*, it's amazing how little he remembers of my various golden words … spoken aloud in the hope they won't vanish forever.

But they vanish anyway. "Marital deafness," he says, though my friends agree it's Bad Memory. Or maybe a male thing, a testosterone-driven ability to tune in or tune out.

If she's gorgeous, he definitely remembers her name and most of what she says.

Rob, in fact, reminds me of the husband of a close friend; she happens to be a charming television personality. Recently, after she'd introduced me to her husband, we wandered into another room and there she said with a smile, "He's deaf in one ear and he doesn't listen out of the other."

After I stopped laughing, I said, "And that goes for my husband, too."

So today, I've just come up to my office to get something. But now I can't remember what on earth I came up for. The letter I just wrote? My class attendance record? Something I left on the floor?

Bugger it, I'm not going to remember, and there's

lots of stuff on the floor, but not THAT—whatever it was.

Anyway, I'm here now, so I might as well sit down and write. The item I needed will come rushing back to my brain fairly soon; the next time I go downstairs it'll strike me, splat, like a bird-dropping on my head.

And that's how our brains function after they've been serving us well for seventy years. They still work. But they're like computers with too many open files.

They're slow.

Lucky for the world, I don't work for the CIA. And you probably don't either. I'm not a medical malpractice defense attorney (like my husband), or an airline pilot, so it doubtless doesn't matter to anyone but me whether I remember the exact altitude of Denver, or how many bones are in the human wrist, or in which month it's predicted that all the computers will fail in Cincinnati. (Or was it Columbus?)

In the meantime, a stuttering memory is merely a nuisance. We're tired of hearing our kids say, before we've had a chance to ponder, "I didn't expect you to remember, Mom," or a friend grinning as he says, "I know perfectly well where I met you—but I'm having a Senior Moment."

In fact, most of us would rather we never again hear the words Senior Moment.

Anyway, in my private estimation I've never been a Senior. I'm just a regular person with a few extra years under my belt. And that's where most of them are. Under my belt.

So what, if anything, can we do to re-ignite our brains? How do we keep them bright and functioning and ready to react at life's most important moments?

For one thing, there's a computer program called Posit Science, a brain-enhancing course for older adults, developed by numerous professors at the University of California San Francisco, at San Diego State University, and at the University of California San Diego. The program was evaluated and tested by MDs and PhDs at universities like Yale, Johns Hopkins, USC, and MIT.

Because the course was considered an experimental study, and thus offered free at the college where I teach, Rob and I decided to participate. As it turned out, the hours we spent there were so engaging and stimulating that we both took it twice.

The time commitment was huge—a total of 90 hours—which translated into four days a week for two-and-a-half hours each day, all in a ten-week session.

Posit Science is a memory-and-hearing course that works through stimulation of the auditory cortex. The designers believe that the memory, the whole brain in fact, of anyone who completes the study will end up being ten years younger—a benefit that does not disappear with time.

Ten years younger! Who wouldn't sit in a chair for a year to end up with a memory on steroids.

Everything depends on us, the students, sitting in front of a computer screen for the requisite hours and listening hard as we react to information that comes to us through headphones.

If the following proves to be Too Much Information, feel free to skip it and go to the conclusion.

Among the six exercises (fifteen minutes each), is the one called High-Low, where you decide whether a succession of little bird-like chirps go up or down. With time they're played ever faster, making them harder to distinguish.

Then there is Story Teller, which is exactly that—a goofy story told quickly and in various voices, with the listener striving to recall minor details. The people with good memories love it.

In the exercise labeled Match It, the listener tries to remember and pair together—then eliminate—matching words hidden under a grid ... made easier if you develop sneaky little systems. (Which I did.) As you work, the grid gets ever smaller, turning the end into a real "Ah ha!"

Tell us Apart means distinguishing words, like "doe" and "toe," that sound nearly alike, but aren't. At first you think your hearing is marvelously acute and this exercise is dead easy. But as the semester progresses the computer-enhanced voice slurs the words so badly you'd swear the designers of the exercise are cheating. There IS no difference, you decide, and what can you do but guess? And it's a pain to guess wrong. Nobody likes this one much.

Sound Replay requires the listener to repeat back a series of sound-alike words—in the same order they were presented. Some of us couldn't remember anything past four-in-a-row.

Finally, Listen and Do means following an ever-longer set of instructions to move little people, like doctors and postmen, around on the screen. You send them from the gift store to the barbershop, to the library, to the ice cream parlor. Rob and I both loved this one.

Altogether, it's very hard work, and while some exercises are less enjoyable than others, none are boring, and the time literally evaporates.

The changes in our fellow students were miraculous. Shy seniors became bolder, people slept better, some claimed they drove with keener attention to the road, many reported they were less apt to lose their keys, more inclined to remember why they went to another room in the house.

Rob and I both felt energized, re-vitalized, if nothing else. We loved both the course and our teacher, and found ourselves pushing other distractions out of the way. We're both so competitive, neither of us wanted to miss a day. Yet the competition was never against anyone else, it was only us competing with ourselves.

On the way home we always compared notes. "I didn't miss a thing in Story Telling," he said.

"And I was a whiz at Match It."

"But how about Sound Replay? I couldn't tell one word from another. "Gee" versus "Kee." Give me a break."

"And today I couldn't remember more than four of those sound-alike words in a row. When we got up to five, I was dead. Dig. Bib. Pig. Fig. Rib. I couldn't make a story out of it, like the pig is digging with the rib, so I stopped caring."

The designers of Posit Science included lessons about other ways to keep older brains young, leaving us with a paper titled, USE IT SO YOU DON'T LOSE IT.

Here, developed by neuroscientists (and stolen— then paraphrased—by me) are their key points:

Choose activities that A. Are challenging. B. Teach you something new. C. Get Progressively Harder. D. "Engage your Great Brain Processing Systems"—hearing, seeing, and feeling. E. Are Rewarding. F. Are Novel or Surprising.

Among the activities they suggest are: learning to cha cha, improving your Spanish, taking up juggling ... all pursuits, they claim, that challenge the brain and get progressively harder.

Our teacher, much-liked Lynda Gunderson, also suggested that we try brushing our teeth with the left—or minor—hand (I still do it.)… that we choose ever more challenging crossword puzzles … that we try memorizing the names of all the people in a new group. To demonstrate, on the second day she amazed us by calling out the first names of all twenty-seven students in our class.

More than once Lynda noted that we could google "Brain Games" and find other brain-challenging programs on the Internet. With a smile she added, "I've played quite a few of them. They're always fun. And some are free."

My own suggestion: that we make it a point to listen. And listen intently. Like the two husbands mentioned here—like me, of course—right in the middle of something, our attention drifts off. And there goes the old recall.

Near the end of the first brain class I tried an experiment. The next time I gave a writing seminar at Leisure World, I forced myself to pay close attention and remember every name around the table—seventeen names in all.

Somehow I did it. (But God help me if any of them had moved.)

AND NOW THE CAPPER TO OUR STORY. DURING OUR sessions in the two brain classes, Rob and I met and became friendly with a number of new people, some of whom I encouraged to join my writing class.

The following semester, on another floor of the school, a new student came up to talk to me. *Darn, you look familiar*, I thought, though I had no idea where I'd last seen her.

"I'm Barbara," she said.

"Barbara?"

"You know, Barbara Simmons."

I'd never heard of a Barbara Simmons—as she knew all too well from the strained expression on my face.

"You know," she prodded. "Barbara Simmons. From the brain class."

"Oh. BARBARA! Of course! How could I forget?" (Actually, I'd never heard her last name.) "Barbara! How nice that you're here."

After she sat down, I thought my students might be amused by the story—how I'd managed to forget where I knew this new student from one of my brain classes.

My students were amused, all right.

And then, from the back of the room, Barbara piped up and said casually, "Actually, I was in both your brain classes."

It was ten minutes before my students stopped laughing.

Chapter Four

Getting Things Open

THE OTHER DAY I HAD A NASTY FIGHT WITH A BAG of peanuts. I was sitting on a plane and starving—with a little bag of nuts that was as defiant as one of my cats, the one that won't let you pet him in the morning. Here was a bag that wouldn't let you break it open—not from the left, the right, nor across the top.

Rob says the core issue was arthritis and I swear it wasn't. It was idiot manufacturing. I'm no weaker than I was a few years ago, and no dumber, either, so surely I can always outwit a mere cellophane bag. (Or whatever it is, technically). *There must be a tiny slit,* I thought, examining the bag from all sides, *or an arrow, or an indentation that tells me where to pull.*

Doesn't every manufacturer offer a clue about retrieving his product? Even if, like my favorite brand of bacon, the clue doesn't work?

Apparently not. There I sat with a clueless bag … and a growing sense that, ounce for ounce, there is no stronger material in everyday use than this peanut wrap. They ought to use it for parachutes.

Finally, with both hands pulling in opposite directions, I tried separating front from back, but the two sides clung to each other like desperate lovers.

Never mind that I consider myself reasonably strong and my fingernails even stronger, the bag won out. Unless I was willing to chew up the package in one lump, cellophane and all, I was doomed to go peanutless.

I looked around for something ... a sharp edge on the seat, a protruding nail, but all I saw with tool potential was the guy sitting across the aisle.

With a smile I leaned across and handed him my little bag. "Please, can you open this?"

He was obviously still in his prime—loaded with testosterone. With a mighty wrench he pulled on the bag, letting only a peanut or two escape before he handed it back, nodding in some kind of personal triumph.

"Thanks," I said. But I was thinking, *Oh, how godly are men. Men who can open things.*

ANY THINKING PERSON CAN SEE THERE'S A CON-spiracy afoot in our country—a conspiracy to make us eat less by making each and every ingredient difficult or impossible to get at. When Rob and I go to a ball game and order a hot dog, I sometimes forget that the mustard comes in flat packets of a few drops each, so you need seven of them … that it takes vampire teeth to make the first puncture, then a mighty twist from what are soon mustard-covered fingers. Then a napkin to remove the portion that squirted onto your shirt. Such is the level of unpleasantness that sometimes, before I order the hot dog, I check out the mustard. If it doesn't flow freely, I skip the dog and go for the ice cream.

The trend toward packaging in open-proof containers is now everywhere. And never mind that I do have arthritis. The last time I bought a curling iron it was sealed up with stiff plastic on the front and impenetrable cardboard on the back—the kind against which even the strongest, non-arthritic hand is useless.

Which goes as well for Rob's new screwdriver, enclosed in a container that required a much larger screwdriver to stab it open—except he ended up using a screwdriver plus a hammer.

You soon realize this problem isn't *us*—*it's them*!

While I was speaking at a conference recently, a woman graciously handed me a bottle of water. But it was one of those newer bottles, with the cap so ultra narrow it provided no place to grip. I had to put it aside and go on talking. As a friend said later, "To drink the water you have to behead the bottle."

The tightly-screwed jelly jar lid is no longer symbolic of all that is wrong with today's industrial packaging.

Rob, no longer a kid (and in spite of sore fingers),

can open the toughest jelly jar with a fierce grimace and a loud grunt. But give him a little squishy container of mustard, or worse, a wrench that is contained within one of those see-through packages—where you can view the tool but never quite reach it—and he's as frustrated as though he was once again a boy of ten.

"It's sealed for the ages," he says, pounding the container with a butcher knife.

Never a patient man, he finally tosses the thing on the carpet. "No sense my trying to open it. They designed this package for the Time Capsule. To break into it you'd need the Jaws of Life."

Few of these problems have much to do with our being Seventy. It's only because of living this long that we've personally witnessed the evolution of wrapping things up—from the simple dropping of merchandise off the shelf into an open brown paper bag, to the demonic packaging of today.

One of my friends noted that you can purchase a special kind of scissors for opening such containers. Which I'd buy, if only they were loose on the shelf. But they're not, they're sealed up like priceless museum pieces. Even my cat, who can dismember the toughest rat, would not be able to reach it.

For you women who don't carry scissors in your purse, you can just forget about the peanuts.

Chapter Five

Weight ... Good, but Could be Better

I THOUGHT MY FRIENDS AND I WERE SUCCESSFULLY hiding our weights and ages—and not with large-veiled hats, either, but with our young-people activities. Some of us still play tennis ... and those who don't do other non-senior things. Most of us still hurry to and from our cars, talk breathlessly at every opportunity, go to movies and plays, make dinner dates with friends.

I assumed we were fooling the outside world.

Apparently not.

Turns out *somebody*—or several somebodies—know all too well the worst of our two statistics: our age.

One day over the phone my friend Carol (whom I've mentioned in other books), was comparing notes with me on the mountain of mail that lies in wait after we return from our trips.

"Before I do anything else," she said, "I separate the mail by category: the political solicitations, the home improvement offers, the diseases ... and of course the ten dozen catalogs."

"Oh, those," I said. "Seems you don't dare buy anything by mail. Or give money to a cause."

Off I went on one of my tangents. "Once Rob sent money to save the tigers. Now we get appeals for all the ailing non-speaking vertebrates on the planet. Blind horses. Crippled donkeys. Starving lions. Rheumatic chimpanzees. Mustangs headed for dog food. Not to mention a 28-year-old tiger with severe arthritis … his caregivers said he was costing them fifty dollars a month. I don't spend that much on my own arthritis."

She laughed.

I added, "I swear we'd also hear from the featherless chickens, except they must know by now we eat them."

"Oh," she said. "There's another category I forgot to mention. The senior stuff. Solicitations for retirement communities, the Neptune Society, hearing aids, and crematoriums." She laughed again. "Thank God I don't need any of them."

So there it was, for both of us. The world KNOWS. They know details about our ages we've never told anyone.

"As for all that old folks mail," Carol observed, "I'm beginning to get the message: Buy Before You Die."

AFTER WE HUNG UP I REMEMBERED THE CARD AN-other friend gave me at one of our all-girl birthday luncheons. The front of the card said, "No need to discuss our ages." Then inside: "I save lying for weight."

Well, at least the outside world doesn't send us ads for corsets, high-protein diet shakes, or bathroom scales. Nobody but my doctor knows how much I weigh.

Oh, and Rob knows, too, but he's too concerned with his own weight to blab about mine.

As a junior at Stanford I was skinny at 150 pounds—in my case, a function of being nearly 5'11" and inheriting my father's big bones.

Anyway, friends at Stanford kept saying I ought to be a model (and never mind my size 10 feet). So during a semester off I went to San Francisco and applied to a modeling agency. They didn't seem to care how my body *looked* ... the people at the agency were all hung up on that 150 pounds. Right away they said I should lose down to 145, fully dressed.

For several weeks I starved myself and starved some more, and finally, just barely, got down to 145, fully dressed. In my underwear standing before a mirror, I looked taller than ever, but now I resembled an anorexic Romanian gymnast.

Triumphant over what I'd accomplished (and imagining the new weight would surely be permanent), I went back to San Francisco and weighed in.

Whatever happened after that has now escaped

me—suffice it to say my body never graced the pages of Vogue. But I do recall vividly that after that fully-clothed moment of exaltation on the scale, I immediately headed for the nearest drug store and a hot fudge sundae.

Soon I was back at Stanford and eating whatever I'd been eating before.

What occurred next was my first big lesson about weight: in only a few weeks I was back to my old 150 pounds—and luckily, no more.

But hey, I was only a kid of eighteen, a student/nerd, if you want the truth, and what did I know then about metabolism, food groups, dieting, sugar, or exercise?

Nothing.

LIKE MOST FEMALES OF ANY AGE, I'D LIKE TO BE thinner than I am. (I'm reminded of that New Yorker cartoon that has a girl baby sitting in front of a mirror. The caption says: "Does this diaper make my butt look big?")

Extra weight is off-putting at best and dangerous to your health at worst.

When you're not looking, extra pounds have a way of creeping up on dark nights and jumping on board. If you don't check often (such as every day), you can discover, to your dismay, that you're ten pounds heavier than the last time you looked.

This happened to me a long while back. For

whatever reason, I wasn't paying attention, merely noticed that certain zippers stopped zipping and some clothes didn't fit at all.

But it was the pictures that did it, the formal photos taken at my daughter's wedding. She looked gorgeous and I looked like Jonathan Winters in drag.

Who was that woman with the puffy face? And why had she worn fire-engine red, for heaven's sake, when she should have donned some dark color that's considered invisible and hidden behind a palm frond?

I was shocked. And so was my bathroom scale. It went up. Then up again. And nearly groaned when it hit 194 pounds.

Even my daughter, always tactful, admitted ruefully, "Mom, you did look kind of chubby."

MY DAUGHTER SAID THIS LATER, MONTHS AFTER I'd taken a private vow: *From now on, I won't eat any sweets.*

All that was a decade ago, and I still remember exactly where I was and how I stared at the green backdrop shielding the tennis court where my grandson was playing a tournament, and how this would not be something I'd talk about to anyone, in case I couldn't do it. Or in case it didn't work.

It was one of those cold-turkey moments—the kind that seem to work best for people who try to stop smoking. You simply stop. You set your mind to NO, and then you turn off the desire button. You shield yourself from temptation. You never look at desserts, not even sideways. You turn your face away when you walk down the candy aisle.

But you don't starve.

Never.

If you're truly hungry, you eat. For most of us, starving doesn't work. Starving diminishes will-power, makes us weak and vulnerable. If we're hungry enough, we'll consume anything, three Baby Ruth bars or the tablecloth.

At Hanoi Hilton in Vietnam, the American prisoners ate rats.

Only when you begin the world's simplest diet—no refined sweets—do you begin to appreciate other foods. Suddenly an apple tastes marvelous. A handful of raw almonds is a better treat than you'd ever imagined. A piece of whole wheat toast with Canola butter and a glass of lowfat milk or a cup of tea with Stevia is a tasty snack.

Unsweetened yogurt with fresh blueberries and a sprinkling of dry, whole wheat cereal is positively yummy.

Tuna fish sandwiches made with a smidge of mayonnaise but generous amounts of mustard, pickle relish and lettuce can constitute a great lunch.

And salads! What would we do without salads?

Salads make the world go round. Salads with dried

cranberries, nuts, celery, mandarin oranges, mangoes, bits of apple and the protein punch of nuts and chicken.

What's not to like about a salad?

DID THE NO-REFINED-SWEETS DIET WORK?

Yes. It did. Absolutely. But slowly. Very slowly.

I'd go down two pounds, up one, down another two, up a half, like the Dow Jones Industrial Average, except that overall the direction was down.

It took over a year; the exact time escapes me. But the pounds came off, and they stayed off. A couple of years later I weighed 174. Many years after that, my base weight is still 174, with a few pounds variation in either direction. If my weight starts to rise again, I react immediately.

As I write this, I yearn to lose yet another ten pounds. Creating this chapter has given me a strong nudge. Okay, it's more like a shove.

HERE'S THE GOOD NEWS FOR DEDICATED sweets-lovers like me (and maybe for some smokers.) After a period of deprivation you no longer crave the bad stuff. Better than that—you don't even think about it. Three days with nary a sweet can be enough to get the sugar-lust out of your system.

The other good news. All other foods now taste better. When you're not eating ice cream, it's surprising how good a slice of mango can taste. Or a whole orange. Or half a steak. Or even broccoli, if it's seasoned right.

AND NOW FOR A FEW TRICKS.

Long ago, when fat calories were the only numbers that mattered to serious dieters—the only calories they kept track of—I discovered that a few tablespoons of Nagano's flavored vinegar tasted as good on my salad as an oily salad dressing. It also improved the flavors of fish, broccoli, string-beans, zucchini, and even baked potatoes.

I began carrying flavored vinegar in my purse, and still do. I found a small bottle with a little bendover, non-drip spout. It doesn't take much space, and I find myself using it constantly. Fat or no fat, I like the stuff. So why not use it?

A second trick. Since I still prefer a sweet taste in green tea, I've been using the natural sweetener, Stevia. For one reason or another, most artificial sweeteners have somehow been discredited. But so far, not Stevia. It tastes good but doesn't increase the craving for other sweets.

Trick number three: Don't eat late at night. Let a few hours lapse between your last meal and bedtime. I've never gone to bed after a heavy, late-hours snack without a discouraging weight gain the next morning. Experts explain that food eaten late at night tends to get thoroughly digested (meaning the transit time is sloooow), so every last miserable calorie clings to your body like Velcro.

The last trick: You must continue eating for pleasure. If every meal becomes torture, you'll never stick to a weight-loss regimen. Find the sugar-free foods you love and eat more of them. And for heaven's sake, don't waste psychic energy counting calories. If you're not eating refined sugar (or consuming piles of French Fries), your calorie count will take care of itself.

Which brings me to my travel agent, Linda, a beautiful woman who seems to spend half her life on cruise ships, heading for exotic ports. Her figure is perfect, and I finally gathered the nerve to ask how she did it.

"Do you exercise?"

"Not much," she said.

"Then how do you stay so slim? With all that cruise ship food?"

She smiled. "Really. It's pretty simple. I never eat dessert."

THERE'S ANOTHER TRICK THAT WORKS ON CRUISE ships: never use the elevator.

For sixteen days on a Crystal cruise to South America, I climbed the stairs—100 steps between decks Five and Ten, which I labored over about four times a day. As on other cruises, I was mostly climbing alone. By the second landing I always had to stop, gasping and puffing, which invariably inspired someone not-on-the-stairs to ask anxiously, "Are you all right?"

Still, the four-hundred steps a day meant I was able to eat ice-cream at dinner—homemade and delicious. Back home again, I'd gained only three pounds.

SOMETIME AROUND MARCH, 2012, THE TELEVISION news magazine, Sixty Minutes, aired a program that should change American dietary habits forever.

Except it probably won't.

Hosted by Dr. Sanjay Gupta, the segment was an expose of the subtle and not-so-subtle influences of sugar (in its many permutations), in the American diet.

To sum up quickly: Various forms of corn syrup and fructose are now so prevalent in everyday prepared foods that Americans are consuming more sugar in a greater variety of ways than they've ever dreamed.

The producers of the program pointed to studies that prove American obesity is less a function of fat than of sugar.

In the end, with charts, photos of overweight Americans, and visual portrayals of MRIs in progress, the producers gave us all a potent takeaway message: sugar is both toxic and addicting.

It was all so depressing I went straight to my refrigerator for some ice cream.

Chapter Six

Hearing Aids—Not For You ... For Your Listeners

I swear, some deaf people prefer to remain that way.

Like my husband claims, "I don't necessarily want to hear everyone's conversations. Most of them are ... face it, Babe, they're boring, not worth listening to." Which may be one facet of his only-child syndrome, his being raised without siblings, so most of those years he listened only to himself.

But of course he's got it wrong. When you're only hearing fragments of conversations, a few words out of every sentence, what remains doesn't make much sense— so naturally the net result is uninteresting.

Try handing me two words out of every sentence and I too will declare the conversation isn't worth listening to.

Which reminds me of the few times Rob has handed me a ripped-out newspaper article, but ripped carelessly, so that all the margin words are missing. They've been among the most boring articles I've ever tried to read.

Anyway, to please me, Rob once manned up and agreed to be fitted with hearing aids. He drove thirty miles to a high-end audiologist, brought home several hearing devices, and finally let me treat him to the most expensive pair, a cool $2400.

Surely, I thought, these will do the trick. They'll make him hear me.

Except they didn't. Rob wore them briefly but, as he said, "All I hear are louder birds, noisier sounds from the kitchen, thundering overhead planes. I don't hear you any better, Babe. And those other noises are just a nuisance." He pointed out that human ears selectively tune out background noise, but hearing aids can't tell the difference. The State of the Union Address or a dog barking—it's all the same to most hearing devices.

He explained further. "I've got nerve deafness, you know. No hearing aids will overcome that. Nerve deafness is permanent. It can't be helped."

And so we left it at that.

Rob and I went on conversing as best we could, with lots of over-emphasized sentences and some hilarious dialogue when he repeated back what he thought I'd said. I once called out to him, "I'm leaving for the store," and he, echoing what he'd heard, said back to me, "You're breathing on the door?"

AND THEN EVERYTHING CHANGED.

Our son-in-law, Brad, found some hearing aids on the Internet. He emailed the maker's name to me (MDHearingAidPRO) but knowing I'd given up, he mentioned them to the only other family member who might be interested—our son, Chris, who also has a hearing loss.

Immediately Chris ordered a pair. But of course he would. Besides his role as a doctor, he's also the gadget king of the family (his television has ten remotes, and his bedroom blinds are motorized). If a gadget has the slightest usefulness, he already owns it.

But here was the possibility of a tool that might do more than all the others.

As it turned out, these hearing aids were a miracle. For the first time, Chris could hear every word his patients spoke. He could scarcely believe it.

Without telling us, he brought them along on our most recent cruise—six family members on a trip to South America. "Here Dad," he said, as he came to our stateroom before dinner. "I've got something you need to try."

"Hearing aids?" said Rob. "Won't work, Chris. I've got nerve deafness."

"Just try them. You might be surprised. If they don't make a difference, I'll just keep them."

Reluctantly, Rob put them on. And then Chris and

I took turns whispering in his ears. First one of us, then the other.

Rob heard every word.

"Where'd you get these?" he asked in amazement.

"Brad found them on the Internet."

"On the Internet? A blind purchase? What's the cost?"

"About five hundred dollars." Chris grinned. "And they come with a year's supply of batteries."

"I'll be damned. What makes these work when all the others don't?"

"They're computerized," Chris said. "Instead of focusing on the wearer's hearing loss, the amplification is set for the frequencies of the human voice. That's basically what you want to hear. All other sounds don't matter."

Rob had a certain look on his face. A look of discovery. Of surprise.

He wore the hearing aids at dinner ... and seemed to hear everything we said. Suddenly, instead of shouting his thoughts across the table, he spoke in normal tones. I stared at him in amazement. This was a brand new Rob.

And so, thanks to a couple of determined relatives who were willing to take a chance, forceful enough to push us a little, Rob's hearing world has changed. Frankly, I love those hearing aids almost as much as I love him.

Only one problem remains. Rob keeps forgetting

to wear them.

He needs to re-read my chapter on memory, but I keep forgetting to tell him.

CHAPTER SEVEN

Exercise: Who Has Time?

YESTERDAY I SAW THE MOST INCREDIBLE SIGHT. My granddaughter's dog, a caramel-colored Siberian Husky outfitted in a harness, pulling her two children up a busy street—her kids happily tucked into a little three-wheel cart. Ages four and six, the girl and boy sat grinning in their funny black chariot while the dog ran gleefully and their mother jogged behind, steering and calling commands.

Clearly, the dog was in his element. He took them three miles, running with spirit and canine bravado, bred to perform just such a task. Everywhere, motorists did double-takes. It was a sight I'll never forget.

JUST AS CLEARLY, I WAS NOT BRED TO RUN.

I may be fighting human nature, but I've never liked exercise for the sake of exercise. I ask myself, What's to like about pushing yourself to run two miles … or struggling to climb four, high-altitude miles to Sequoia Park's

Heather Lake … when all along your body is protesting, *What are you doing to me? Why is this supposed to be fun? Stop it right now!*

Like some authors who don't like to write but love HAVING WRITTEN, I don't like heavy exertion, but relish HAVING EXERTED.

Still, stubborn German that I've always been, if I start a long hike I usually finish, because then I can gloat to myself—or anyone who will listen—*I just climbed to Heather Lake.*

Years ago I often jogged two miles on the high school track. I pushed forward on reluctant legs, exhorted them to perform, but I never really liked it. And they didn't like me either.

For reasons I've never understood, my daughter—and assorted granddaughters—seem to crave actual pure exercise, like the one who runs behind her dog, or another who goes on two-mile sprints through Peters Canyon, or my daughter and her friends taking five-mile power hikes up and down the grades in Lemon Heights. For all these endeavors I'm happy to applaud. I just don't want to do it.

BUT THAT'S ONLY ONE KIND OF EXERCISE—THE exertions which to me seem boring and awful, even painful.

There's another kind I love—exercise with a purpose.

For fifty years I played tennis, and as long as points are involved, along with gamesmanship and strategy, and a lot of team spirit, and human brawn versus human brains, I'm there. I'm in. I'll run as often and as hard as the game demands, take lessons to improve my serve, do backhand drills against a backboard … whatever it takes to win matches and become a better player.

It seems easy to appreciate the exercise involved in team sports, like water polo and basketball. Less easy to understand how an athlete browbeats his body into grueling solo pursuits, such as field-and-track, competitive swimming, gymnastics.

We know about the swimming, saw it first hand. One of our sons, Kenny, was both a high school and UCLA swimmer in the butterfly. While he was still living at home and churning through endless laps before and after classes, all he did in his at-home hours was eat.

In my minds eye he is still there at our breakfast table, broad-shouldered and wasp-waisted … gobbling down food, and still more food.

The eating I understood. All those laps in the pool, I never did.

Oops … i've forgotten to mention my love of skiing … and ice skating. And bicycling. And dancing.

But it's coming back … memories of what it's like to ski: the joy of the long, graceful slide down a snowy slope, the sensation of being so light on the earth that you're nearly airborne, the wind in your face, the graceful turns, almost like dancing, first in one direction, then with a slight exertion of knees, a swoop in the other, but still sliding, skimming above a snowy surface, becoming a feathery creature that is gently gliding down. Ever down.

Lovely moments like these are surely considered exercise after all—but only when they end. How could I forget skiing?

Why didn't I think immediately of ice skating?

Or dancing? Or riding a bicycle?

All with the same exhilaration as skiing.

BUT NOW COMES SEVENTY ...

Suddenly there's a new perspective on exercise—the gerontology police wagging fingers in our faces, exhorting us to get-up-and-move ... lest they find us, some day, limp and lumpy in our Barcaloungers. They insist we be out on the sidewalks thirty minutes a day, six days a week, walking, always walking, like hamsters on a treadmill.

Some also mention weight-training and muscle workouts, in case plain old walking isn't enough.

Sometimes I wonder—how much exercise was done by long-lived Winston Churchill?

Not very much, it seems. Acerbic as always, he once said, "Whenever I feel the urge to exercise, I sit down and wait until the urge passes."

Regretably, most of us are no longer part of the exercise world we once dearly loved—the tennis, the skiing ... or even the dancing. We don't have the muscles we used to have—or more important, the balance. We get out of breath.

So maybe we should listen to the experts and make time for those daily walks.

But where?

I've already seen all the flowers in my neighborhood, I know our sidewalks intimately, and I don't need to keep looking at houses I've already seen. For me, walking just to be walking becomes exercise for its own sake, the boring, mindless activity that's so hard to like.

For awhile, I did this my own way. I read books as I walked—really read them—or critiqued student manuscripts, which changed the experience, made the exercise seem positively engaging. I knew my sidewalk's peccadilloes, its occasional little dips, the uneven edges, the breaking away for curbs. I never tripped, never ran into anything.

But I became something of a sideshow. People kept pointing me out. "Oh, you ... you're the lady I've seen walking down Browning, reading a book. Isn't that dangerous? Aren't you afraid of falling?"

"Well, maybe," I say. "But so far I haven't." I tell them I've memorized the sidewalk, know all its little idiosyncrasies, such as where the curbs drop off, so I know when to look up. In fact my only near-misses were with unseen people coming the other way. Suddenly there they were, staring into my face. But we never collided, because at least one of us was looking.

EVENTUALLY I GAVE UP THIS … WELL, LUNACY. It began to seem too crazy to continue. Instead I substituted other routines.

Exercise now comes in several modes … and they have to be pleasant or I won't do them.

The first is a stretch, flex, and breathing routine, which I do on the floor, technically called "Body-Flex" and orchestrated by Greer Childers, the author who introduced them in her book, "Be a Loser." (People tell me it's another form of Yoga.)

My husband bought the book for me when it first came out, in 1998. Now, fifteen years later, having done them nearly every day, they've become what I call my "Huff and Puffs."

When I first began, our grandkids were fascinated, especially by routines that involved weird faces and strange noises—the out-loud puffing combined with one's chin elongated and tongue sticking out … or the one with face pointed at the ceiling and lips formed into a snout. "Do it again, Grandma," they clamored, and they'd try a few imitations, except right in the middle they'd start laughing and couldn't finish.

Childers promised her faithful followers an extravagant loss of inches (with no diet), which for me happened only in my thighs. Instead, her routines worked other miracles, like keeping my back free of pain (when x-rays say it's a mess), and making me flexible enough to touch palms to floor without bending the knees—such a way to impress your friends.

My son Chris apparently mentions the book to his orthopedic patients, because he called some time ago asking for the title.

Whatever the routine does or doesn't do for health and lumpiness, it seems worth the paltry twelve-minute expenditure of time. Not only is it something you can do anywhere, such as on a hotel bed, or on the carpet in front of the television, but it makes you feel virtuous.

So now, with stretching and breathing handled, what can be done for cardio-vascular conditioning— sometimes called aerobic exercise—or just cardio?

How do we cope with boredom, which is probably the number one excuse for abandoning a program?

Two ways work for me: a stationary bike and a treadmill. And both are twofers, offering exercise combined with mental stimulation.

And by the way, stationary bikes and treadmills are usually available on sites like Craigs list, leftover from all the people who liked the idea of working out but not the working out itself.

Since you won't be bothered by cars about to run you down, you can safely read on your stationary bike—even without a book rack. Miles-wise, I've probably pedaled to Canada and back. And read a bookcase worth of books.

With the pedals set at low resistance, it's possible to hold a volume and read as you pedal.

Or, in my case, I critique student manuscripts, pausing only to scribble comments in the margins. Once you're used to pedaling, you can carry on indefinitely—at least until your bottom gives out. Which reminds me, I must get a new, softer seat, since my current limit—before numbness and/or pain sets in—is about twenty minutes.

The other enjoyable form of exercise is reading on a treadmill ... overall a more demanding form of exercise. As with the stationary bike, you can set the machine for any speed, fast or slow. But for reading you need a book rack.

The limitation here is that ordinary print is too small to be seen on a fast-moving treadmill, even when you're holding on with both hands. But The Reader's Digest has solved this problem with a Large Print version of the magazine, plus their newer, Large Print books. (And other Large Print Books are also plentiful at the library.)

We subscribe to both ... and I soon discovered the

better the book the longer I walked. While a tedious story may be good for ten or fifteen minutes, a real page-turner can pull you along for thirty. In fact, with a great book, I've been known to re-set the timer past thirty and keep treadmilling and reading.

But books aren't the only distractions that make treadmills and exercise bikes bearable. There's also television—which many a devotee of staying fit uses to make the time go by quickly.

It's only fair to mention swimming as a pre-ferred form of senior exercise. (For me, this doesn't work. We don't have a pool and I'm too fussy about my hair, which requires a half hour's work after a wetdown.)

But for people without hair issues, swimming may be a top exercise contender. Certainly the gerontologists love it for being low impact, and so do seniors who've always relished moving through water.

A last thought about walking: the most ef-ficient walks I've ever taken were those when I grabbed a head start from somewhere close to home and tried to beat my driving husband back to the house. Or those few occasions when I was so mad at him I stomped out of wherever we were and left him without a word and walked home alone—just to "show him" of course. (A temper tantrum which he pretends not to notice.)

Clearly, these were "motivated walks," the kind that aroused my competitive spirit. Very aerobic, but not the kind I'd do every day.

Still, if I'm ever invited to run behind a Husky pulling little kids in a funny black cart, I might just do it.

CHAPTER EIGHT

Travel: A "Mixed Bag" Means More Than Your Suitcase

FOR YEARS ROB AND I WERE VACATION SNOBS. WE thought that people who traveled in large, organized groups, herded on and off buses by brisk, peppy troop leaders carrying flags, required to appear at breakfast by seven a.m.... . were simply mindless sheep. We wanted none of it.

Instead we often found ourselves in foreign countries like Austria or Italy at dusk with too much luggage, no place to sleep, the wrong money, and unable to say more than "Thank you" in the language.

This was our idea of Adventure.

It was also, quite often, the source of some upsetting early-evening hours, not to mention significant marital strife. "*I told you*, we should have gotten off the train while we could still see!" That would be me.

"And I'm telling *you* to relax. Take a pill."

"What do you mean, relax? How do I relax on a

bench in a train station?" Then under my breath, "I'm going home!" *Yeah, like how? It's not like I can walk.*

Eventually, things always worked out, and we now have memories of places like the private home in Austria, where the mother had on display a medal for producing babies for Hitler. She acted sheepish, but not sheepish enough to take it down. We remember luscious country breakfasts where egg yolks were the color of ripe oranges.

We recall a rambling hike in Austria with a jolly Austrian who poked fun at the grim approach taken by visiting Germans. Pointing to a distant, very steep mountain, he said, "Ach ... over there are the Germans. Every day climbing up. All the time falling down!"

We spent a dozen evenings in cozy English pubs "chatting up" the locals, a day hitchhiking in a dairy truck across the English Moors, hours spent bicycling in Scotland, an afternoon playing tennis in Majorca—with who else? ... a couple of Germans.

I kept trying to keep score in German, but I'd get no further than "Ein Schwein," before they'd start laughing. I soon learned I wasn't saying, "One, two," I was saying "One pig."

Like others our age we booked coach airplane tickets and thought nothing of it. The price was controlling: cheap was the goal. We bought Britrail passes and Eurail passes, and rode trains everywhere, getting off sometimes by design, often on a whim.

Looking back, we both now agree—most of it was fun.

But that was then. Escapades in the 1960s and '70s.

Since those halcyon days more has changed in the travel world than just us. Whoever heard, back then, of long, tedious lines in airports to make sure that you, and other Seventy-year-olds like you, are not carrying explosives? Especially in your shoes?

Who would imagine it would not be physically possible in some of America's larger airports to walk from one gate to another? That to make it in the allotted time you'd have to hop on a train—or run?

We have a story about that. Only weeks ago, five younger family members arrived in Dallas on a much-delayed plane. Knowing their time for the connecting flight was nearly gone, they alerted the man at the nearest gate to radio ahead to the plane's captain, and then they began running. All five churned through the airport like Olympians—at top speed.

Gasping for air, they arrived at the correct gate, only to find it already buttoned up. Nobody would open the doors to let them on. My daughter said, "We stood at the window looking out, and there was our plane, still sitting there, not moving. It sat for fifteen minutes—plenty of time to let us board. So what was it waiting for?

"Finally we saw our luggage arrive. Our stuff went up the ramp into the belly, and then finally the plane left. Without us, of course."

WHO WOULD HAVE DREAMED, BACK IN THE SEVEN-ties, that America's long-distance carriers would stop offering coach passengers free food? Or that airplane manufacturers would squeeze up the coach seating space until there was no longer room to cross your legs? My friend Pam describes how she does it. "With both hands I lift my leg way up high, higher than the seats, send it out in the aisle, and finally pull it in again over the other leg."

Who would have guessed you'd be charged to check your suitcase or—as on a few airlines—that you'd be charged to put luggage in the overhead bin?

REMEMBER WHEN GETTING THERE WAS HALF THE fun?

Then you must be Seventy—because today it isn't.

But then we've changed too. We don't run like we once did. (The truth: we don't run at all).

Thank god for wheels, because we can no longer carry a small suitcase, a drink, a lunch, and (for me) a purse. Unlike our kids, we can't cross half an airport at warp speed. We would have missed that Dallas plane, whatever its captain chose to do.

These days we're acutely aware of what can happen with long, coach-induced sits. We think about blood-clots.

With airports now so spread out, we've just discovered, on one of our rare coach trips, that there's seldom enough time to pause between planes and buy last-minute food.

Sure they give you peanuts. But speaking for myself, they can't be opened. (See Chapter 4—peanut bags from hell.)

STILL, FOR US IN OUR SEVENTIES, THERE ARE SOME mostly-good options. We travel less than we used to, but now we plan ahead, using credit-card miles to upgrade. Thanks to being retired (at least Rob is retired), we can be flexible about scheduling. No early-morning flights and ragged first days. First Class on most airlines is still pleasant, roomy, and offers nice meals—several notches up from those once offered by coach.

Since we're no longer the hikers, the chance-takers of yesteryear, we're not into bumming around foreign countries, hauling luggage and taking pot luck on accommodations. Now we take cruises.

Cruises? Us?

As Rob says, "Never, in my wildest imaginings, did I see myself as a cruiser. Never thought I'd let others control my destiny. Couldn't picture myself joining forces with all those white-haired people."

But then, he never saw himself with white hair ... or using a cane. And he certainly never guessed that most of the women would sport hair that was every color but white.

Since his first exclamations of denial, Rob has come to love cruising. No hauling luggage. No packing and unpacking. No scouting for meals. No getting stuck in strange cities with inferior places to sleep, like lumpy beds and smoke-tainted rooms. If he goes at all, he splurges on the best accommodations we can afford.

Even traveling by ship, we've visited plenty of exotic cities—Copenhagen, St. Petersburg, Helsinki, Tallin, Stockholm, Buenos Aires, Rio de Janeiro, London ... the list goes on.

We usually bring younger relatives who help with luggage ... and we let our much-traveled son-in-law treat us to between-plane stops in American Airlines Admirals Clubs.

Furthermore, we walk as much as we have to, and sometimes more ... but we're not forced to run.

With those uncertain security lines, we no longer take chances on missing planes.

WHICH REMINDS ME OF THE THINGS WE USED TO do ... traveling for his company, Petrolane, Rob once drove all the way to Los Angeles (an hour each way), but missed the plane. The next day he drove back, encountered even heavier traffic than before, and missed the same plane again. He says now, "This makes me sound like a moron."

Looking back, we were ... well, nuts. In those days the two of us were so often late and irresponsibly last-minute, we usually found ourselves running through LAX just like our family, desperate and winded, spoiling the start of many a journey. On one trip we didn't stop panting until we were over Denver.

On a flight to Hawaii, once, we showed up in such anguish and so out of breath, they actually took pity on us and upgraded us to First Class.

EVERYTHING WE ONCE DID HAS CHANGED. You might say Rob and I are finally gaming the system, that we've figured out how to have a great time in spite of added girth and greater hassles. We've grown used to the bad parts and now kid around with those who could make us miserable, like the people in TSA.

Rob, the once-great adventurer, now likes travel somewhat less than I do. But we're both making it work. And most of the time, though we're not necessarily thrilled, we're at least satisfied.

So what's wrong with being Seventy?

Chapter Nine

Curing Your Colds—From Me and Linus Pauling
(But Probably Not Your Doctor)

Laugh all you like, but I'm positive chemist Linus Pauling was right: vitamin C does cure colds. Though with one additional wrinkle ... *you also have to give up refined sugar.*

If you read about him on the web, you'll see what I mean. Or you might take my word and let me share what I found.

During the mid years of his career, Linus Pauling was renowned world-wide for being the chief advocate and guru for vitamin C, for his assertions that high doses could cure cancer, heart disease, and the common cold. Yet this eminent scientist, the only person to have won two unshared Nobel Prizes—the first for Chemistry and the second for peace—was debunked in his later years as a quack.

Surely, thought doctors of his era, the claims that

Pauling was making for a lowly vitamin as a possible remedy for such divergent afflictions could not be true. To prove their point, the National Institutes of Health (NIH) conducted a series of experiments which seemed to discredit the Pauling conclusions and put them to rest for all time.

Yet certain literature was still out there, vivid testimonials that supported Pauling's assertions, all waiting to be validated by yet another team of scientists.

And even I, who am no scientist, have had personal evidence of the miraculous powers of vitamin C.

Before you snicker, remember the uneven history of most medical breakthroughs: the doctors who derided a colleague for washing his hands between delivery of one baby and another; the surgeons who were slow to accept Dr. Joseph Lister's methods for preventing post-surgical infections; the controversy in the medical community over Louis Pasteur's radical theory that germs cause disease.

And now I quote from an article entitled, "Linus Pauling was Right All Along. A Doctor's Opinion."

"When they examined the evidence, Drs. Steve Hickey and Hilary Roberts found background evidence for Pauling's ideas from independent scientific and medical reports, covering half a century. The findings in these papers could neither be dismissed as placebo effects nor easily explained. The reports included remission of AIDS, cures for cancer, and the immediate recovery of children at the point of death from septic shock. The claims seemed so out of the ordinary that they were hard to believe. However, Hickey and Roberts could find no counter examples in the scientific or medical literature."

To Roberts and Hickey, the only contrary message came from the NIH's data on blood and tissue saturation (of vitamin C.) Closer examination by these doctors proved that the NIH conclusions were not correct. The two studied the NIH experiments and found them to be full of errors.

The article concludes that Linus Pauling may yet prove to be a man who was years ahead of his time, that the world of medicine may eventually discover that Pauling was right after all.

So why do I jump through such elaborate hoops before relating my own experiences with vitamin C?

Perhaps it's because my husband, a medical malpractice attorney and a virtual dictionary of medical information, thinks I'm a quack.

But it's also because my son, an orthopedic surgeon, prescribes vitamin C for all his post-surgical patients. "And," he says, "I think my patients have fewer infections than would normally be expected."

SO HERE'S MY STORY.

Years ago I found that I was often able to head off a cold by taking large doses of vitamin C while the cold was still in its infancy.

It didn't work every time. But on some occasions the vitamin C was practically a miracle. I'd be on the verge of a cold—scratchy throat, a general sense that I'd soon be ill—and I'd take heavy doses of vitamin C (1000 mg. every two hours for half a day) and sure enough—suddenly the cold was gone. No sniffles, no fever, no cough.

The problem was, the cold was usually caught so early that I couldn't prove to anyone, including myself, that I was really going to be sick after all.

So how could I claim I'd discovered some kind of medical miracle? Besides, since my "cure" worked sometimes and not others, my evidence was ... well, lousy.

But I did notice one thing: if I managed somehow to veer away from refined sugar, the vitamin C was more apt to work. If I resumed my usual consumption of ice cream and See's candy, all was lost: the symptoms came rushing back.

There were times when I found myself on a virtual roller-coaster between "cure" and illness. Vitamin C and no sugar—cold goes away. Introduction of sugar—cold comes back. More vitamin C and no sugar—symptoms subside. At times it was uncertain which outcome would prevail. All too often I couldn't give up my sweets and I ended up with the cold.

A theory began to form. Maybe heavy doses of vitamin C only "work" in the absence of refined sugar. Maybe it's a two-pronged requirement, one dependent on the other, which the medical world knows little or nothing about.

But how could I prove anything, now that I hardly ever caught a cold?

Then one day recently, along came a strange opportunity. Without warning, I was suddenly sick. By that I mean seriously sick. My throat was raw, my epiglottis swollen, my body feverish. Clearly, the illness was too far advanced for any miracle vitamin cures. This would be a cold I'd have for weeks—and I'd be coughing for a month.

Knowing there was no chance in the world that vitamin C would help, I nevertheless began taking big doses. One thousand milligrams about four times a day. And for once I avoided sugar. I mean all of it. Didn't come near it, nary a bite.

By the end of the first day I felt somewhat better. So I went on with the program—big doses of C and still no sugar. By the end of the second day I was markedly better. But I didn't let up. For two more days I kept up the routine. But by the end of day three I was entirely well. All signs of the cold were gone. I'd gotten sick on a Monday and by Wednesday I was cured. No runny nose, no cough. Nothing.

This time there was no doubt in my mind about where I'd been headed. I'd gone miles past a scratchy throat, straight into big time illness. But somehow my double-edged plan worked.

For once, what had happened was no longer a question. I celebrated with anyone who would listen, meaning three or four people. And I suddenly remembered that on prior occasions I'd often taken chewable vitamin C tablets, which are made palatable with sugar. The current tablets were un-sweetened, in fact quite sour.

My husband still thinks I'm a quack. He thinks big doses of the vitamin are toxic.

My doctor son says they're not toxic.

Just recently, in answer to my question, our family doctor looked up vitamin C on her pharmacology data and also found it to be non-toxic.

In the meanwhile, I've interviewed a friend who was a classmate of Rob's and is now a judge on the ninth circuit, clearly an intelligent woman. We chatted about my books, and then about the issue of vitamin C. She said, "I've been taking it for years. A 500 mg. tablet in the morning and another at night."

"Do you have arthritis?"

"No. And I've never had a cold that lasted more than one day. If I start to feel sick, I double up on the C and it goes away."

She mentioned that she also believes in the power of cold-water swimming … and afterwards, a hot water Jacuzzi.

So you, the reader, can believe whatever you want. All I can say is, four weeks ago my husband came down with a terrible cold. He took one dose of vitamin C and then stopped. He didn't give up sugar. The miserable, drippy part of his cold lasted a week and a half, leading him into bronchitis. A doctor finally gave him antibiotics.

Now, four weeks later, he feels all right—except he's still coughing.

I kept expecting to catch his cold, but somehow, with lots of hand washing, never did.

Anyway, I wasn't particularly worried. My reasoning was based on one powerful anecdotal experience, but for me it was enough.

Chapter Ten

Driving—Determined to Get There

Like most type-A personalities who think they can accomplish two day's work in half a day, I'm always in a rush.

Which fits perfectly with the rest of the driven, type-A syndrome—being delusional about time. We imagine, for instance, that just because we can shower in under five minutes, it's possible to go from nightgown to gas pedal in under fifteen.

As Type-A's we tend to overlook the everyday realities that might slow us down. Like ringing telephones (which we always answer), wiping down the shower, applying deodorant and face cream, choosing an outfit, fluffing the hair with extra curls, then discovering that a nylon sock, already halfway up the leg, has an unsightly run … and that's before we leave the bedroom. Further into the house there's feeding the mewing cat, putting away the milk, unhooking the cell phone from its charger, telling our spouse the three things we forgot to mention earlier, then returning to the house for the three things we left on the drain board.

In a ready-to-go state I've often left my computer, gone down the stairs, and headed straight for the car ... only to discover it took thirteen minutes to actually get there. (Some people can jog half a mile in that time.)

Sure, time evaporates. But never as fast as it does in the space between your bedroom and your Prius.

For speeches, class, and doctor's appointments, I always allow extra time. (Well, not so much for doctors). But it's never enough. By the time I'm backing out of the driveway, whatever I'd previously considered "extra" is all used up. I'm now running on less-than-extra.

So there I am in my trusty Prius ... rushing.

And that's when the safety mantras begin. *It's the last half of the yellow light: forget crossing the intersection.* Who needs a time-wasting traffic ticket? (And oh Lord, I just noticed the cop waiting at the light.)

Hold the left turn; you won't beat that car. You want to REALLY lose time? Try having an accident.

Don't panic about missing the turnoff. So you missed it. Too late to swerve over. Take the next exit and come back. What's five extra minutes compared to a freeway pileup?

With luck you'll drive twenty more years; don't blow it now.

Such are the mantras that run through my head as I push the Prius to get me to my class on time.

Mainly, I want to arrive. Intact.

So I curb myself. All the way to the destination this little tape runs through my brain, annoying but constant, comparing the ten minutes I'm running late to the time I'd lose if I did something stupid.

And then I find myself thinking about my ten young grandkids, all of them now driving cars, and I'm musing to myself, *I hope a few mantras are running through those kids' heads*.

At last a final mantra: *Dear Lord, forgive us our lateness, for we know not what we do.*

Chapter Eleven

Eating Out, Guilt Free

Hate me if you want, but I don't iron clothes and I hardly ever cook—at least not much beyond breakfast. Like a retired dentist who never wants to see another gaping mouth, I no longer want to hang around in an ingredient-filled kitchen. These days it's hardly a kitchen, anyway, it's more of a snack palace.

Once you've mothered six kids, five of whom were perpetually-hungry boys, further duty over a hot griddle seems about as appealing as ... well, as cooking on a boy scout campout, where you start by rubbing two sticks together. I've earned my Get-Out-Of-the-Kitchen Free card.

Of course we still have to eat. And never mind that my husband's first question of the day is invariably, "So, Babe, what's the plan?" Meaning, what have I planned for breakfast?

A strange question for a normally bright man, but he's never figured out that I haven't planned anything.

It's not D-day. Breakfast has never required an all-out assault ... so there's no need to make lists and consider nutritional values and ponder ingredients and compare today's possible offering with what we ate yesterday.

I just do it. Spur of the moment. We either have eggs in the refrig or we don't. I either make a creamed corn omelet or egg and toast or hot cereal or whole wheat pancakes or bacon, eggs, and potatoes or toast and peanut butter.

Depending.

Unlike me, *he remembers what we ate yesterday.*

Rob's the one who says, "It's Wednesday, Babe. That's pancake day," as though Wednesdays are not within our control. As though midweek pancakes are a dictate handed down by some powerful unseen entity—the breakfast god, I presume, or whoever he imagines rules our kitchen.

So yes, I cook breakfast. Beyond that, the kitchen is closed.

WHICH LEAVES A COUPLE MORE MEALS.

Well, one actually, because the two of us have figured out that after you reach Seventy, three whole meals in one day is one meal too many. The trick is to eat a late breakfast and an early dinner, and in between to simply reach out your hand for whatever is closest—some nuts, or a few strawberries, or raisins, or—god forbid—some potato chips.

And now, about four hours earlier than what would be considered normal in sophisticated-eating countries like France, Rob and I go somewhere for dinner.

Or sometimes I bring something in.

But, except for momentous occasions, we don't do expensive. To tell the truth, we don't even *like* expensive. I, especially, am turned off by huge slabs of beef, even well-marbled beef, blackened on the outside and bleeding on the inside. It's simply not appealing to eat something that appears not quite dead. Or something that might have perished in a fire.

As Woody Allen says, "I want my food dead, not wounded."

On the other hand, better cooks than I are everywhere, dishing up great varieties of fish (which I never do at home), or chicken served with sauces beyond my imagination, or salads with luscious ingredients I wouldn't know where to buy.

We go to Soup Plantation and load up on lettucy things, or to Boston Market for luscious sweet potatoes and barbecued chicken, or to H-Salt for fish and lightly-battered zucchini, or to Mimi's for their special hibachi salmon with brown rice.

Happily, vegetables are served everywhere. No need to bring home big cello-bags of prepared carrots (and end up eating half), or whole red peppers, or massive heads of broccoli. Someone else will cook them—maybe not perfectly, but good enough. At most of these places, the price for both of us is under $20 ... a mere start at the grocery store.

The calories work out all right, too. If the serving is sized for the gifted, overweight eater, you bring part of it home. Mimi's hibachi salmon is somewhat pricy and high in calories—but not when you're only eating half.

So for dinner, Rob and I mostly eat out. My excuse is that I'm a writer, not a cook. And Bob's is that eating out is his best chance of achieving that second meal.

Chapter Twelve

Sleep: Truth and Consequences

I have to hand it to babies and old people. They really know how to sleep.

Like others in my age group, who of course are not old, it seems I've forgotten how. I keep telling myself, Babies can do this. How hard can it be? *Really, Maralys, there's nothing to it.* You just turn out the lights, close your eyes, relax a little, and think pleasant thoughts. You fake a yawn.

And nothing happens. You are not transported into The Land of Nod. Or anywhere else.

After a short time, when your left shoulder starts aching, objecting in a mean-spirited way to carrying even the slightest weight, you roll over and try the other.

Still nothing. Except while you're not sleeping you've come up with a good opening line for a chapter. And a long to-do list for tomorrow.

So you get up, take a pill and, while it's deciding whether to do its work, you make the list and start the chapter. Before you reach the second paragraph, you're sleepy and back in bed.

Five hours later, when you wake up mid-slumber, you're granted another opportunity to work on the chapter.

Thus go the nights. Ten hours consumed getting eight hours sleep. But eight hours if you're lucky.

EACH NIGHT IT'S A NEW BATTLE. *I'm taking no pills tonight. I don't want to become an addict. I'm no Michael Jackson.*

Instead of pill-popping, you conjure up sleep-inducing schemes. Alternate plans like a half hour on the treadmill. Once in bed, counting slowly with each breath, maybe to a hundred. Or a simple acceptance of the worst possibility of all: No sleep.

I'm not alone in this. One of my friends, a pill-less kind of woman if there ever was one, told me the other day, "If I don't get enough sleep I'm useless. Unable to do anything the whole day. But one good night and I roar around the house and yard like there's ten of me."

Exactly.

"So how do you solve this?" I ask. "Do you take pills?"

"Of course. When nothing happens, I take a Halcion."

"Oh, really!" *Suddenly I'm feeling worlds better.*

Until then, I'd imagined myself as the only

pre-addicted soul in our group. And never mind that none of my doctors blink even slightly when I admit to my on again/off again sleeping pill habit.

When it comes to sleeping-pill addiction, it's each man for himself. With or without help, you take yourself down—or you don't. You pay attention, watch your doses, try not to get desperate, once in awhile let yourself go sleepless. So you lose a night—and afterwards a whole day. Your reward will come shortly. The next night you'll sleep like ... well, like a baby.

YEARS AGO, SLEEP DIDN'T SEEM ALL THAT IMPORT-ant, at least not to one of us ... I recall a few overnight trips to Las Vegas that Rob took with colleagues (while he was still working for a corporation.) With one of the casinos sponsoring the trip, a TWA Constellation plane with piano bar picked up the group from Long Beach airport and delivered them back early the next morning.

They spent the night gambling in glitzy casinos. Once Rob found himself sitting at the next table to Elizabeth Taylor. In sum, it was twenty-four hours, all without spending a minute between sheets.

And then there was another nightclub event which I shared with Rob in Tijuana, when a "free spirit" friend slipped a Bennie into his drink and he danced all night, seemingly without consequences. Since I wasn't given one, I was both astounded at his endurance. And miserable.

For reasons I never understood, Rob held up all right after those occasional events, tired only for a day or two but afterwards perfectly intact.

None of this would have worked for me, at any age. Even as an eighteen-year-old at Stanford it became obvious that before an important exam extra sleep worked better than extra studying.

In fact, with adequate sleep I was ten times better at everything.

Thus, at an early age I became something of a sleep-aholic. As Rob says now, "You slept all through our marriage."

Huh!

Just today a male friend described the perils that accompany a "mixed marriage"—meaning, in the context of this chapter, when a morning Lark marries a night Owl. "At ten p.m." he said, "I'm ready to hit the hay. God knows when my wife comes to bed. Next morning she'd sleep 'til noon if she could. We're hardly ever awake at the same time."

Now, at seventy, we sometimes sleep when we don't want to. At lectures. In movies. In front of the television. You could say we sleep around. Literally.

Twenty years ago I had a preview of Sleeping in All the Wrong Places. Rob and I belonged to a group

called the World Affairs Council, a gathering which con-
sisted of couples whom we perceived at the time as so
ancient they could have voted for Hoover. I remember
how warily we approached the dinner tables on meeting
nights (we were always late), looking among the sea of
gray hair for someone with the color brown. And finding
none, how pleasantly surprised we were that everyone at
our table was lively, interesting, well-informed … and
probably no older than we are now.

As one of the group's special projects, a public rela-
tions event, the United States Strategic Air Command
invited one member from each of twenty families to view
Offutt Air Force base in Omaha, Nebraska. Rob chose
me as our family's designated visitor.

As I look back at myself, I was basically a kid—at
least compared to the others. With a friend's husband I
drove to March Air Force Base, for our required arrival
time of 4:00 a.m. Our flight was on a military DC-10,
highlighted by a mid-air refueling, with a view of the
refueling plane up close and personal from a rear window.

Once at the base, we sat down for the first of several
"briefings." In a luxurious room with soft leather chairs,
an officer turned the lights low and began a Power Point
presentation, describing for our benefit the mission of
SAC.

I promptly fell asleep. A short time later when I
awoke, I looked around. Except for the man who was

lecturing, not one person in the room was awake. I only slept for ten minutes. The rest of our group, in their comfortable chairs, snoozed through the entire presentation.

I like to pretend there's a difference between a tiny nap and an all-out Rip Van Winkle slumber. But that distinction was probably lost on our hapless presenter.

Now that I've demonstrated I can sleep anywhere except in bed, I struggle not to be the person at our Discussion Group who quietly nods off during the discussion.

In fact, for Rob and me, sleep these days is a practical joker, keeping us awake at night and too often dozing during the day.

No longer do either of us agree to be anywhere before 11:00 a.m. Rob, as always the owl (who sneaks short naps in his special, TV-viewing chair), is seldom in bed before one a.m., and seldom out the next morning before nine. Whereas I, who'd be a morning lark if I could qualify, find myself still awake at all kinds of crazy hours … often because I've broken one or more of my own rules.

Here they are. I don't claim these mandates are original, only that I've learned them the hard way.

1. No caffeine after 3:00 p.m.--which includes coffee, tea, and sodas. Caffeine has a way of "hanging on"—with a longer afterlife than you ever imagined. And while we're talking caffeine, there's plenty to be found

in that best of all yummy desserts—Haagen Daz coffee ice cream.

2. No rich chocolate cake, chocolate candy bars, or chocolate anything late at night. Besides sugar, chocolate also has a stimulant, xanthine. The stuff will make you feel terrific—and you'll be awake to keep feeling terrific for hours. You might as well abandon your bed and go somewhere to read up on Nutrinos.

3. Make time for physical exercise—but not right before bed.

4. Don't think late-night liquor will make you sleep. It won't—at least not soundly.

5. To keep them working, don't take whole sleeping pills, like Restoril, oftener than every other night.

6. On "off" nights, maybe take half a Halcion to get back to sleep after a middle-of-the-night wakeup. (Okay, it's a sleeping pill too).

7. When various body parts are really hurting, it's okay, according to my rheumatologist, to take half a Vicodin. But be aware that Vicodin takes at least half an hour to start making you feel better—and drowsy. And often, consumed without food, it can give you a stomach ache.

ALONG WITH THESE RULES, MY DOCTOR SUGGESTED the first of several "tricks." "At bedtime," she said, "You might try a tablet called Melatonin. It's a simple, non-prescription, non-addictive natural product. Be sure it's 5 milligrams."

I tried it, and while the results weren't spectacular, it seemed to ease me into light sleep … at least part of the time. And the druggist assured me it could do no harm, even in conjunction with a sleeping pill.

The second trick is a middle-of-the-night thing. It's a sometimes solution for that aggravating mid-sleep wakeup, when your mind jumps to full daytime alert. Instead of drifting off again, you're mulling over tomorrow's speech, the bills you forgot to pay, better strategies for winning at Sequence, the friend you never called back.

You're now so wide-awake you could go fight a forest fire.

Instead of ruminating, try rolling over and creating images in your brain. Recite mental pictures to yourself. "I see a cloud drifting across the sky … a plane flying low … a village down in a valley … people walking across the square … a lake in the distance … a telephone pole … a rabbit running nearby …

If you manage to conjure up, actually "see" five images in a row, you'll be asleep.

To make this technique work, you have to concentrate. Force out all competing thoughts, push hard to bring up a series of soothing images, and keep reciting them to yourself … (and God help you if your husband chooses that moment to cough.)

For me, this succeeds about half the time. I'm aware that it's work, intense mental effort, that it takes willpower ... that I simply cannot allow myself to think about anything important.

Hours later, when you realize you've been asleep, you feel like rejoicing.

ON NIGHTS WHEN NOTHING WORKS AND YOU MUST resign yourself to being tired the next day, try catching up on no-brainer chores—like paying bills or cleaning out the junk drawer.

Or just sit like a lazy lump and finish that not-so-good book. Maybe those boring sentences will offer exactly what you need: an unexpected nap.

Chapter Thirteen

Grandkids: Your Newest Pals

YEARS AGO I NEVER IMAGINED I'D BE "GROWING MY friends"—as though I was planting little seedlings in a garden, like carrots, and tending to them and nourishing them so they'd grow up and be my buddies.

But that's kind of what happened. Grandchildren are easy to regard as ... well, grandchildren, but only for a fixed amount of time, only until they reach their early twenties.

After that, they're one of us, one of our friends, meaning they've become people we like to meet for dinner, or play games with, or just hang around with. You know, like our other friends.

With me, particularly, this weird thing happens. I keep forgetting which generation these kids belong to; I actually find myself equating them with their mothers and fathers—as though we're all of an age, except that some of us color our hair and others don't.

I mean, if you can talk to the person one-on-one,

if you can let him or her drive you around without any qualms, if you feel the same about politics and global warming and treating all races the same, if you can confide in this grownup person your private worries and aspirations, even accept occasional advice ... what age does that make her?

Actually, it makes my grandkids generationless.

I think the same goes for Rob—that he sees them through the same funny eyes that I do.

WE'VE TRAVELED ABROAD WITH FOUR OF OUR TEN grandkids. Our granddaughter, Christy, at age fourteen, led us through the "tubes" of London's underground as though she knew exactly where she was headed. Rob and I had to scurry to keep up. "She does know where's she's going," said Rob, "and we've been here a dozen times."

"I can't believe this, Rob. But hurry. She's moving fast, we're losing her."

A grandson and his wife accompanied us on a British Isles trip, on which my grandson, Brandon, said to me in Scotland, after I'd dipped my fork into his plate for the tenth time, wanting to take "just one bite": "Grandma, your stomach is now a cornucopia of one-biters."

THIS SAME GENERATIONAL MELDING WORKS FOR other families, especially for one of my best friends,

Elaine, who regularly takes her grandkids to sophisticated places—to New York City, to Hawaii, to first-run plays, to concerts, as though no generational gap exists.

Actually, I adore two of Elaine's grandchildren—the only two I really know. And I suspect she feels the same about a couple of mine.

Just last week I celebrated my birthday with Dane, the grandson who was born, as I was, on July 6. How vividly I remember rushing away from my birthday luncheon with friends to see him arrive.

For years now we've been sharing our big day—he bringing a few of his friends, and I with some of mine. Dinner is outside on our patio, where we tell stories back and forth as though no age differences exist.

On this last occasion I asked the sixteen party guests to tell us about their most memorable birthday. Dane started his story with a grin. "You all know how competitive I am." (He plays volleyball at UCLA). He began telling us about his tenth birthday when his mother (our daughter), suggested all the young boys play games—for substantial prizes. "She let me choose the games," Dane said, "and also choose what we'd win. Naturally I picked stuff I really wanted. And then for weeks I practiced. When my birthday actually got there, I won every game."

With impeccable timing he waited for the laughter to subside. "My Mom didn't see this coming. She made me give all the prizes to the other kids."

Now that our children are clearly through having children, we'll have to "grow" some great-grandkids.

CHAPTER FOURTEEN

Making Habits Work for You

FOR TOO LONG I'VE BEEN WALKING LIKE AN APE.

It's true. Ever since my second knee replacement and the months of favoring the weak leg, my everyday stride has deteriorated into an unsmooth, bobbing, shoulder-dipping set of motions, the kind you'd see in the jungle. Not quite knuckles dragging on the ground, but not pretty, either. Not how I'd like to walk at Fashion Island.

Still, my means of locomotion kept escaping my attention—that is, until various people asked, "You're limping, aren't you?" to which I replied, "No, I don't think so. At least not intentionally."

But then I saw my reflection in a store window. You ARE limping! *This is not good. You look awful. Surely you can do something.*

Well, surely I could try.

It became apparent right away I'd need to develop whole new patterns ... and changing such a basic habit as everyday walking is tricky and not easy to come by.

First you must figure out how to do it differently. How do you alter your stride so it's normal-looking, no longer the lumbering walk of a tipsy orangutan?

You try various things, but none of them make much difference, none of them "take." The old, awkward way is still sticking fast.

You analyze. So what part of your body needs to do something different? What part of you is responsible for walking? Uh … not your shoulders … not your arms, not your head. It's your LEGS!

You walk with your legs—and nothing else. You stride out, all legs, nothing else moving. Because, damn it, nothing else HAS to move.

As I tried walking differently, a mantra formed in my head. WALK WITH YOUR LEGS! WALK WITH YOUR LEGS! WALK WITH YOUR LEGS!

With each stride, I said the words in my head, WALK WITH YOUR LEGS, which seemed to conform nicely to the motion itself, and suddenly I WAS walking with my legs—and nothing else. The rest of me wasn't moving—and I was standing straighter. For a few minutes I could do it perfectly.

But the next time I stood up to go somewhere, it was the same old rocking motion. So I stopped. Repeated my mantra, and set off afresh.

Now I say it to myself every time I walk. WALK

WITH YOUR LEGS.

Sometimes I forget to say the words, then realize the legs are performing quite well on their own, thank you. They've developed a new habit, a new muscle memory. They're making me walk like a normal human being. Straighter. Smoother.

It's been a month, and the habit hasn't fully hardened, isn't yet set in cement. Occasionally the legs and shoulders revert, send me back into the old rocking motion. But now I catch myself immediately and the mantra does the trick.

And so it goes with habits. If you really care, you can make them work for you. You can leave the jungle.

IF YOU STOP TO THINK ABOUT IT, HABITS GOVERN a huge percentage of our everyday lives ... How you drive, how you dress, how you put things away, how you converse, how you eat.

For example, when you go to a potluck, how much food do you normally take? Lots of everything, so you end up with a heaping plateful? Or one tablespoonful from each dish?

Those of us who have switched from the heaped plate to the one spoon are now eating half as much. And oddly, we don't miss the extra food. Nor is it something we think much about.

Where do you put your car keys? Always in the

same place? So you're not wasting energy on frantic, last-minute searches? Years ago in Discussion Group, a member remarked bluntly, "If my car keys aren't on the bureau, I'm not home." The group laughed ... but now, years later, Rob and I both recall the aggressive way he said it.

When you undress, where do you put your clothes? As a teenager, I dropped them on the floor. But the mess became horrific ... and anyway, I learned it took only seconds to hang them up. Our dressing room is testimony to two sets of habits: the hang-up side and the floor-dropping side ...

Rob and I are the Felix and Oscar of closet decorum.

Where do you store important papers? In our family it's Rob who learned early to set up new files for new topics, so he can easily find whatever records he needs. Here I'm the bad one. I store important papers in piles until I can no longer find anything ... or until the pile topples over, whichever comes first. Like Rob with his clothes, I make periodic efforts to organize important papers. And sometimes I actually succeed.

In the meantime I simply lament that I will never enjoy the luxury of a clean desk. But as best-selling author Jeffery Deaver said, "I love being a writer; it's the paperwork I can't stand."

HABITS, LIKE SOME PEOPLE, CAN BE TRICKED, EVEN

permanently fooled. For instance, a TV news item noted that if a restaurant serves the diner a whole sandwich, he'll probably eat it all. But let them cut it into quarters, and most people will eat only three.

Likewise, when I spoon up ice cream directly from the carton, (have you noticed I love ice cream?) I'm apt to keep eating, scarcely aware of how much I've consumed. By habit, I now scoop it into a bowl—so I can SEE the total amount.

Savvy dieters, relying on habit, serve up their food on small dishes—a way of fooling their eyes into thinking they have a full plate. These same people tend to use smaller forks, resulting in smaller bites—but lots more of them. Another habit that seems to work.

LIKE MOST PEOPLE, I'VE DEVELOPED HABITS I'D like to change. Most irritating is wandering through the house carrying a paper that I need to set down while I do something else. Once the sheet is absently placed on a little-used spot, it sometimes takes hours to re-locate. Recently I did that with a filled-in check … and didn't discover it until days later, sitting on a box of fliers.

Now before I set something down, I go through a little mantra: YOU ARE PLACING THIS LETTER NEAR THE LAMP BY THE COUCH.

Changing one habit would please me more than most—remembering to ask friends and acquaintances about their lives, instead of rattling on about my own. Over and over I've been surprised and delighted by stories I hadn't known existed—because I simply forgot to ask.

The more I work on this habit, the better life gets.

Chapter Fifteen

Paying Attention to Your Body

SOMEWHERE THERE'S A CARTOON THAT SHOWS A woman lying in a coffin. Her face wears a resigned expression and out of her mouth floats a message: "I told you I was sick."

Clearly it's a lament designed to bolster the psyches of a lot of defensive hypochondriacs.

Of which I am certainly one. At least that's what my husband and my doctor-son think. But it's okay, they say. It's definitely okay. Because such an attitude has served me well.

Over the years I've learned not to let strange symptoms go unheeded. I pay attention to my body. And never mind that it's sometimes embarrassing to mention this little ailment, or that small, growing lump, and risk hearing, "Oh … you again? What's wrong now?"

Always aware that I may appear foolish, I report the problem anyway—because I'd rather face health problems head on and be wrong, than ignore them and end up later with a disaster ... with that thought bubble above my head.

So I am something of a hypochondriac. But not a total, hopeless case. Not a weirdo.

I don't make up strange symptoms. I don't search around for evidence of disease. I don't see problems where none exist. The truth is, I consider myself basically healthy, reasonably fit, and mainly focused on issues other than health.

Lately, I've even felt annoyed and impatient as I read some of the health bulletins that regularly come to our house from prestigious universities like UCLA and Harvard. Who wants to keep worrying about all the physical problems that might, eventually, do you in?

Better to spend your psychic energy in other places, like keeping up with friends, becoming a better wife, ratcheting up your teaching skills, writing a better book, trying to elect the right people to represent you in Washington.

If you want the truth, I'd rather NEVER think about my health; it's a boring topic—except when it's terrifying.

But the problem is, I read too much.

I'm all too aware that ovarian cancer is a silent killer. I know that women can experience pain in strange places like shoulder, jaw, and neck and not realize they're having a heart attack. I've read that people spread more germs by shaking hands than from any other form of social contact, and that the most germ-ridden spot in a hospital room is … no, not the bathroom … but the remote control for the television.

Anyway.

Here's how one small symptom, easily ignored, ended up saving my life. It was after one of my knee-replacement surgeries that, while still in the hospital bed, I put on my bra and accidentally left it on for the night.

Next morning when I took it off, my left breast was a tiny bit sore—but the other wasn't. Not a big deal, really. Just something I noticed.

Home again, I asked Rob to take me for my overdue mammogram. He did, and the results should have been reassuring because the technician reported that my pictures had proved negative and everything was fine.

Yet somehow I still had this niggling suspicion, enough to make me look further. So I went to my regular internist, who gave me a thorough breast exam and said he didn't feel anything. Afterwards he said, "If you're still not sure, you should probably go see Dr. West at the breast care clinic."

Soon Dr. West was doing a fine-needle biopsy—inserting a needle into the left breast. The procedure was painful, but once again the result was negative. Still, just to make sure, he also did an ultra sound.

And there he saw it. A small lump. "But I don't

think it's cancer," he said. "My guess is, it's benign."

"Shouldn't we take it out, though?" I asked. "Just to be sure?"

"That's what I'd suggest."

A short time later I was in surgery. When I woke up, my husband was by my bed, and so was my beloved daughter-in-law Betty-Jo, looking down at me tenderly. "It's cancer," she said. "The lump was cancerous." But the way she said it, with such warmth and tenderness, made the problem seem minor, made me feel I'd be okay.

"Dr. West took it out," said Rob. "He had to put you down deeper, Babe. Actually, he was quite surprised."

So that was it. I'd been right to persist. I'd paid attention to my instincts, instead of assuming mammograms are always accurate, and letting the diagnosis wait for another year.

All the facts resolved in my favor. We'd caught the cancer early. I didn't need chemo. The only remedies were a course of radiation and five years of taking the drug Tomaxifin.

Now, nearly ten years later, there's been no recurrence.

But that's only incident Number One. The second occurred many years later, the time that I felt, again as a niggling sensation, a strange "pulling" in my groin. It didn't bother me much, and I would gladly have ignored it. But having read about the silent deadliness of ovarian cancer, I thought maybe I should check it out.

So I went to my Ob-gyn, who did various tests which ended with an oopherectomy. When she found nothing serious, she said, "You ought to have a colonoscopy."

Two procedures later, another doctor found a small, easily-removed colon cancer.

So here was another surgery, this time with no need for further treatment. As it turned out, the "pulling" sensation had been adhesions from a long-ago appendectomy. Without them, I might have waited indefinitely on the colonoscopy.

THE TAKEAWAY HERE IS TWOFOLD: YOU SHOULDN'T spend lots of valuable energy worrying and fretting about your health. You shouldn't be constantly checking out your body lest you find a single note that's out of tune.

On the other hand, when something definitely seems amiss, wait a bit and see if it goes away. If it doesn't, have it checked by a doctor. You'll be left with one of two results: nothing was wrong, so you can stop worrying. Or something WAS wrong, but you caught it early.

From all these experiences, there's one thing I've learned: Being half a hypochondriac can save your life.

Chapter Sixteen

Burning Bridges

As far as I know, all these years I've burned only one bridge. And I didn't exactly burn it, a fellow writer did it for me. I remember the day all too vividly, how after church my once-friend suddenly decided to tell me off in the sanctuary courtyard saying, among other things, that I was "histrionic." Not a label I'd ever heard before, at least not attached to me.

I was so shocked I couldn't respond ... beyond shedding a few tears on the way home.

As an author it's easier to collect your wits over a keyboard, meaning your best responses, your real zingers, are reserved for paper ... leaving the merest hope that someday the other person will find them.

When I thought about her later, how this meek and whispery person, the very soul of reticence, had lashed out, I felt like I'd been attacked by a butterfly.

Proof that she lived in her own, made-up universe came a few weeks later, the day I sneaked into church late, stooping low to minimize my lateness. I sat down quickly, looking neither left nor right, trying to be invisible.

Moments later I was aware that someone in the row behind me was getting up to leave. A quick backward glance showed me it was her, scurrying away like a rabbit.

Later, she told a mutual friend she considered my choosing the pew in front of her "an act of aggression."

All I chose, of course, was an empty pew. The open-warfare-in-church bit was in her head, like a scene from one of her romance novels.

Since then, although I've tried once or twice to say hello, she's found me invisible. Not easy to see past someone who (in spite of shrinkage), is still nearly 5'9". You might say that bridge has definitely been burned.

OVER THE YEARS I'VE WITNESSED A LOT OF BURNED bridges, almost all with great tolls in human happiness—most of the perpetrators hanging on to stiff-necked pride at the expense of peace and tranquility. Turning their backs on joy, when a few healing words might have brought them renewed love.

Pride instead of happiness—it's an exchange I've never understood.

Two of my good friends have daughters who have chosen, inexplicably, not to speak to their mothers. In both families important anniversaries and momentous occasions have been celebrated without the all-important daughter, leaving a gaping hole in the mother's psyche.

Still, both mothers have continued reaching out to their foolishly angry daughters. As far as the rest of us are concerned, both mothers could win honors for the qualities of their parenting.

Another friend chose, for twenty years, not to speak to her son. When at last they reunited, it seemed to the rest of us that they'd wasted twenty precious years.

BURNING A BRIDGE WITHIN THE FAMILY IS NEARLY always tragic. But burning lesser bridges can be nearly as bad. I did something I regretted for weeks—sent a strongly-worded email to my editor when the cover on my newly-arrived book was not what I'd hoped.

I should have waited until morning. I should have held the email and reconsidered my words ... taken a second, more thoughtful look—at both the cover and my opinion.

That was when I realized the most dangerous word in the English language is "Send." Unlike a letter, you can't grab it off the hall table and re-write it. You can't tear it up and start over. The match is struck and the fire erupts before you've even sat back in your chair. Now, with today's modern technology, bridges can be burned in record time.

I was so chagrined I sent both flowers and candy.

The editor forgave me, but I learned a stark lesson. Now, for anything important, I never touch "Send"—not until I've waited a few hours, re-read my words more than once. It's a dangerous button, that one. Right up there with the one in the President's red briefcase. Because it doesn't give you a second chance.

Beyond such hasty bridge-burning is the all-too-human proclivity for jumping to conclusions—thereby burning a bridge based on false information. My husband and I nearly did that over the invasion of the bees.

On the far left side of our house a hive of bees had set up housekeeping and caused beehive problems, among which were bees in my office. We hired an expert to get rid of them, but to no avail.

Finally the next-door neighbor phoned to say that her husband was allergic, and could we please do something. We tried again, with other experts, but the bees kept returning, clocking in both at my office and the hive.

One day an animal-control woman from the county appeared at our door. "Your neighbors have complained about the bees."

"Which neighbors?"

"I'm not allowed to say. But I'm here to ask that you resolve this problem." There was an "or else" implied in her tone.

Rob was instantly angry. "I can't believe they called the county. They know we're trying to get rid of them." Hostility colored his tone, an assurance that these neighbors would now be our enemies.

I listened to Rob rant most of that evening, before I finally decided next morning we should face the problem head on. I called the neighbor, found her home, and explained all that had happened.

"But I didn't call the county," she said, bewildered. "I'd never do that. We've been friends for too long."

I took a deep, relieved breath. "Oh, I'm so glad. It didn't sound like something you'd do." Actually, I was overjoyed. "Rob will be happy to hear this."

That evening her husband came over to further explain that neighbors like them don't call the authorities on neighbors like us. They resolve problems face to face.

From that moment our friendship grew stronger.

As if I needed the lesson, I realized how right I'd been to investigate before I let myself get angry. How dangerous it was to jump to conclusions and go flying off the handle ... especially when you might be wrong. I wasn't Seventy for nothing.

The friendship was rescued, but not our problem with bees. We hired other experts, now five in all, and at last the problem seemed diminished.

I wrote the county woman a letter, outlining our five-expert attack, then ending with the words, "We're still making an effort. And the critters are still trying to defeat us. Please understand: bees will be bees."

"Take that last bit out," said Rob. "If we end up in court over this, that sentence won't look good."

"But it's funny."

"That's exactly what I mean. To the county, this is not funny. It's serious business."

So that letter became one more bridge I didn't burn.

CHAPTER SEVENTEEN

Organ Recitals

SOMETIMES WHEN I'M RUNNING SHORT OF BOOK material, Rob steps up to supply a topic. After all these years he's still my biggest supporter.

For this book he said, "Babe, you should have a chapter called Organ Recitals."

I stopped to think. "I'm not sure there's enough to talk about. What can I find to say?"

He tried to be patient. "You're writing a book about old people … the kinds of things they talk about. Here's a great topic. Besides, it's potentially funny."

Funny? At that moment I drew a blank the size of Alaska. You can't be funny when you have no thoughts on the subject, when you can't even conjure up a first line. I stared into space.

"It's obvious," he said. "Do you want me to write it for you?"

I shrugged. "Let me remind you, Rob … we don't consider ourselves old."

"Well, you and your friends must talk about something. I say it's Organ Recitals."

And thus I began.

WHEN YOU WERE IN YOUR THIRTIES, WHAT DID YOU imagine that people in their Seventies talked about?

I know ... their ailments. "Oh my God, you should have seen the size of my kidney stone. I could have played golf with it. The doctor says I have the biggest scar he's ever seen. Here, you want to see it?"

My husband calls these conversations Organ Recitals.

Odd as it seems, I've never been to an Organ Recital. Nobody in any group I've been part of has spent even a minute talking about such invisible items as their livers, gall bladders, kidneys, stomachs, or ... God help us ... their bowel movements.

Apparently the people in my groups don't have organs, they're traveling through life organ-free.

However, I have been part of many a broken-bone, sprained ankle, pulled tendon recital ... as of now reserved for people who have yet to reach their thirties. A grandson shattered his elbow jumping a motorcycle, another sprained his ankles several times playing volleyball, and a granddaughter destroyed her hand when her bicycle—not moving—unexpectedly tipped over.

Eventually older age groups got involved. My

daughter, well past forty, has pulled ligaments and tendons playing tennis, and my son, Chris, temporarily tore up a knee falling down some unlit, outside hospital stairs.

Rob and I each have two fake knees; actually, they are real knees, just not the original factory equipment. So if you include discussions of these external members, maybe I have, after all, been part of some serious health talk. But this is not typical of our group's conversations.

So what do people in their Seventies talk about?

Everything.

Give me an important topic and we've discussed it. Global Warming. Income Disparity. Alternative Energy. Presidential Races. The Supreme Court. Unusual Weather. Wildfires. Civil War in Syria. Joe Paterno and Penn State. Congressional Lobbyists. Political Shenanigans. Good and Bad Parenting.

And various not-so-important topics: Celebrity marital scandals. Good and Bad Writing. Good and bad food. Good and bad movies.

If any of these topics brand us as "Old," then the entire nation is old.

So today I declare that the topic of "Organ Recitals" is now officially closed. And thus retired.

MEANWHILE: HAVE YOU HEARD ABOUT HOW SCIentists have developed tomatoes that are guaranteed red, but have no flavor?

You haven't? Oh, don't get me started on that topic. I could go on and on …

Chapter Eighteen

Friends: The Sine Qua Non of Happiness

My friends and I grew up together. Which sounds like an exaggeration, except it happens to be true.

As I think back, four of us have known each for at least fifty years … which makes two hundred friendship years. In the early stages of our lives we all played tennis, and though the game has faded as an element of sisterhood, it was tennis that originally brought us together, and the same sport that in some ways subtly defined who we were.

Back then, two of us played with fierce, tournament-focused determination, while the other two approached the game with more humor and insight but less competitive spirit.

Patty, in fact, played mostly for fun. But even she developed a wicked, underhanded serve that had a nasty habit of unfolding where it was least expected—usually right down at the opponent's feet, practically on top of their shoes. Most of us stood there openmouthed as the ball floated over the net, then suddenly unwound and dove into a death spiral, then ingloriously died.

As her partner, I often pleaded with Patty, "Get out that serve. Now! We need it!"

Just as firmly, Patty refused. "It's unfair," she said with a laugh. "I can't do it to them."

"But it's our secret weapon."

"That's why I won't use it."

So one of us, at least, would not bring out her deadly serve to win … the only Ultimate Weapon among the four of us. For Patty, victory was secondary to friendship.

For Carol and me, victory on the tennis court was a separate issue. For an hour or two we played with concentration, focus, and effort, racking up all the points we could. Neither of us were maniacs … we never cheated, were never unpleasant. In fact, we laughed a lot. But we also wanted to win.

Off the court, neither of us cared much how it all came out. "When it's over, it's over," she said. "I go on to other things."

"I'd still like it better if we'd won," I said. But then I, too, managed to put the loss aside. At home I was deep into writing another book.

For both of us, tennis was just one facet of our lives—but a segment we loved for all the years we did it.

Elaine fits a separate category. More competitive than Patty, less than Carol and me, she and her husband,

Marty, carried tennis rackets to Kauai, and with the two of us played couples' doubles. Elaine and I wanted to win ... oh, we certainly did, at least for the moment. "Come on, Maralys," she said, "You take the net, I'll stay in the backcourt and do the running." And then, "Maybe I should try your racket. Here, let's swap."

"You think it'll help?"

"I don't know. But we need to try something." We did a quick exchange. "We can't let the guys take us."

Gamely, we fought off the two men as best we could, each of us playing with rackets we weren't used to.

"Ah well," she said after Marty and Rob prevailed. "We'll just have to beat them at Password."

We look back on those years with nostalgia—and now sadness, because Marty is no longer with us.

I can't imagine life without the rich addition of friends. I've never laughed so hard or so often as I have with my three best friends (and a fourth who is now deep into Alzheimer's), or felt so young after a three-hour luncheon that was fifty percent laughter, fifty percent touching on serious subjects, and zero percent organ recitals, back-biting or cutting up other friends. (Our jabs were strictly reserved for politicians.)

Long friendships are the gift of remaining in one area for many years ... and long friendships, obviously, cannot be established late in life, on short notice. Like diamonds, old friends take a long time to make. The years you've shared together are simply there—the past is on file—with no need to relive them as you'd do with someone new.

THE DEEP FRIENDSHIP AMONG THE FOUR OF US BEgan casually nearly fifty years ago—but suddenly became more serious when one of us developed agonizing problems at home. A call was made to the other three. "Our friend is in trouble. We need to have a summit meeting." And so, starting that day twenty-seven years ago, we formed a permanent sustaining support group.

Meeting regularly for lunch, the three who were happy with their lives provided avid listening, encouragement, bits of advice, friendship ... but mainly bursts of laughter for the one who wasn't.

At times the woman in trouble said, "I wouldn't have survived without you."

"Oh yes you would."

"No, honestly," she said. "I couldn't have made it. The three of you kept me going. This is the only place I've been able to laugh. I go home feeling happy again. Years younger."

In time that person's agony subsided, but the group remained. Eventually the rest of us had our own painful issues ... with grown children, with grandkids, with in-laws, with health concerns ... and eventually with the deaths of two husbands. Yet the summit group endured as an entity—a bastion of support and a permanent fountain of laughter.

As we increasingly found ourselves unable to tear away from animated conversations, the luncheons stretched out and today are seldom fewer than three hours … until, by the time we leave, we're the only diners left.

Now, as though the intervening years were a mere blink in time, we still meet at the same high-end restaurant at least four times a year. The waitresses know us, accept the fact that we always choose the same table and invariably sit in the same chairs.

More often than not, when we're ordering food one of us will say, "I'll have what she's having." An old joke, of course, but it defines us.

As much as I love my husband, one of the strongest threads in my life is this group of four women. Rob knows this … and thank heavens he accepts it.

My daughter, too, has a similar group of friends. A larger number than ours, usually eight women, they've known each other since they all lived in the same neighborhood and their children were babies. The group began in Irvine, California, formed as a mothers' baby-sitting co-op.

No longer. The members have largely moved to

other states, but this has not stopped them from getting together once a year in one or another home … and in a variety of places. They've been to Texas, Colorado, Arizona, and Nevada. "You know, Mom," said Tracy, "our group is amazing. In all these twenty-five years, none of us have had money problems, only one child has dabbled in drugs, we've had no divorces and no marital strife. How often would a group this size be able to claim that?"

Tracy describes her get-togethers as I would describe mine: "We spend hours laughing. We all tell intimate stories—but we've never had anyone get angry or upset. By the end of the three days we all feel renewed, as though we could take on the world. It's the kind of energy that keeps you young."

With men, groups like this are rare. Yet they exist—though perhaps at a lower level of intimacy. We just had lunch with an eighty-five-year old … the contractor who, fifty years ago, built our house. Even today he is fearless and strong, able to climb a very tall ladder to seal off the bees from Chapter 16 who are still trying to invade our house.

Glenn's wife died a few years ago. Now, every Saturday morning he and a group of four or five men meet for breakfast. His expression as he talked told me his male friends fill an important role in his life—in a way as important as our women friends do for us.

And then there's Air Force Veteran Harry Page, 89, who once a year unites with fellow Air Force pilots from World War II ... a group that understandably grows smaller with each reunion. He said, "We meet in different cities every year. When we get together, all we talk about for three days is the war. It's kind of disgusting, but it's true."

Two years ago the group met in Omaha, Nebraska. But Page's wife of 64 years was ill and he hesitated. He said, "I won't go this year," but she said, "Oh yes you will." His daughter overheard the conversation and decided to accompany her dad. "Before we were through with the convention," he said, "my daughter knew more people than I did."

A few months after they returned, his wife died.

Since then, the Air Force alums have met in Washington, D.C., and this year in October will convene in St Louis. "Originally," Page says, "we had 5000 men after the war. Now we're down to 50 guys for the reunion. They all bring members of their families. My daughter and husband are going with me this year. Last year it was my grandson and his wife who went."

The bond uniting the group has lasted more than sixty years. We women can only guess at the emotional pull that emanates from war, at the power it exerts over the men who fought together. Stronger than any woman's group, these bands of men will remain united until the last one is gone.

THOUGH NONE OF MY CORE GROUP ARE KIDS, new-er friendships keep forming for all of us. And we all wel-come them. These days, a strong sense of kinship lasting five or six years begins to seem like an "old" relationship.

Happily, I've formed more than a dozen such liai-sons—with long-time students, with some of my daugh-ter's friends, with wives of men we've seen professionally, with people who've joined what we call our "Discussion Group," with members of my charitable groups, even the renewal of some older relationships with couples from our church and tennis club.

With less energy than we once had, we seldom en-tertain at home, but nobody minds. Going out to dinner is easier, more relaxing, and no one kicks you out, even if your group is the only one left in the restaurant.

AMONG THE PEOPLE I'VE INTERVIEWED FOR THIS book, the most recent was Dottie Jackson, a ninety-year-old woman who was traveling alone on our plane to Texas. (Ultimately, we went on to the Virgin Islands.) As with other older people I've talked to, the subject of friends came up often.

The youngest of eight children, Dottie was trim, al-most skinny, and nearly wrinkle free. She was traveling to Dallas to visit a friend.

"How do you feel about your life?" I asked.

She smiled. "I've always been happy."

Then she added, "I lost my husband when he was ninety. He worked 'til he was sixty-two, then we traveled for 10 years. But I got tired of playing, so I started keeping house again. When my husband got ill I had to puree his food. By the time he died, I'd lost twenty-five pounds."

She took a deep breath. "Life is what you make it. I stay busy. I take joy in the simplest things. I've got a pacemaker and stents. My doctor says it's medicine that keeps me going." She grinned. "But every time I see him he calls me "Miss Fantastic." He says, "Don't change a thing."

"Do you exercise?"

She nodded. "I used to walk two miles. But I still walk half a mile a day in the neighborhood. Besides that, I'm on the run all day long."

"At home, do you still have a social life?"

"Of course. I'm a greeter at the Methodist Church. Years ago I formed a group who regularly goes out to lunch. It's now down to two. But we still do it."

She added, "My neighbors are wonderful. We all have good times together."

"Do you have children?"

"No. But I have nieces and nephews. I'm making a blanket right now for the newest great grand niece. The ones nearby I call my California Kids. One of my nieces comes over every night for dinner. I love to cook, and I especially like to experiment. So I cook for her."

She turned to me with a grin. "I bake a special, no-name cake. I'm famous for it."

As a final note she added, "I still drive. I'm going to drive until I die." Then with a laugh, "I'm a better driver than half the people on the road."

"I feel good about myself," she said. "Confidence is one of the most important attributes you can have."

As far as I could tell, in spite of being a widow, in spite of being held together with stents and a pacemaker, Dottie was among the happiest people on the plane.

Chapter Nineteen

Medications: Pill Popping Scenario

For many of us, the pills begin piling up long before we're Seventy. On television Big Pharma pushes its products relentlessly … *are you having trouble sleeping, breathing, playing with your grandkids … are you "ready" when it's time to make love?*

If you're a man, do you spend too much time at the urinal? As a woman, are you (ahem!) constantly rushing off to pee?

We have the answers. Ask your doctor and he'll prescribe the pills.

Pharmaceutical companies are diabolically clever when it comes to figuring out which ailing viewers are likely to watch which television programs. Their ads are forever in our faces and, like Australian black flies, we can't get rid of them.

Unfortunately, Big Pharma is not given to telling plain truths: half our pill-popping could be eliminated, if only we'd do something simple—like lose twenty or thirty pounds. (Okay, it's simple but not easy) … if only we ate more of the right stuff, and less of what harms us.

If only.

BESIDES ELIMINATING THE NUMBER OF PILLS WE take, a good diet and reasonable exercise could help eliminate the number of doctors we visit.

The pill-popping problem is illustrated by a scene played out recently on television:

A doctor walks into his aging father's bedroom, glances at the old man's bureau, and begins examining vials. He shakes his head, astonished. Along the top is an array of pills so large and varied it appears the old fellow went crazy in a pharmacy.

With rising concern, the doctor looks them over one by one, putting aside first one vial, then another. Eventually he winnows the collection down to two or three bottles and dumps the rest in a big sack.

The narrator on television points out that this is an all-too-common scenario. Elderly patients with a variety of ailments are seen by one specialist after another, each intent on prescribing a different drug … but none aware of—or told about—all the other medications the fellow is taking. (Perhaps the doctor asked, but the patient just couldn't remember.) In the end, the hapless patient ends up swallowing them all.

The doctor in the scene speaks up. "My father has

been taking at least three medicines which are either complete duplicates, or not meant to be taken together. It's a wonder he's not sicker than he is. With most of these gone, he will begin to feel better."

To understand why America is known as a nation of pill-poppers, try visiting the Orange County Fair, where you can order deep fried hamburgers at the aptly-named Heart Attack Cafe. An hour of watching the crowds as they lumber by says it all: obesity, at least at county fairs, is rampant. The slim, normal-weight person is almost an anomaly.

Rob and I go every year and never get used to the spectacle, which is both alarming and sad to watch. The average obese person seems to fall into the range of 50 to 75 extra pounds—and some, the morbidly obese, a great deal more. Bellies hang over belts, rear ends waddle, one overstuffed leg can hardly make it past the other.

A great many souls are so large they can't even walk, and ride around on motorized wheel chairs. We can only guess what they must be eating.

But one thing is certain, most are taking pills for diabetes, hypertension, heart disease, high cholesterol. Or they're being diagnosed with cancer.

Food at the fair is a cardiologist's nightmare. Last year as we chatted with a fair employee, he told us about the strangest of all offerings. "Did you know they've got a booth selling deep-fried butter?"

Rob and I did a double take and began to laugh. "Come on," I said. "You're kidding."

"Never heard of it," said Rob. "I'd have to see that to believe it."

"I'm serious. The booth is right over there." He pointed. "Honest-to-god, they're offering it, just like I said!"

Of course Rob and I had to go find out for ourselves. And sure enough, high above the little stall was the confirming sign, Deep Fried Butter. As we watched, the cook ladled a glob of stuff out of a bubbling vat of oil—something with a crusted exterior, and inside … well, I guess it was butter.

THIS YEAR THE FAIR HELD A SECOND SURPRISE. After I told our butter story to Brad, my son-in-law, he said with a grin, "they also have chocolate covered bacon."

"Really?" I said, and made a face.

Rob made a face.

Our granddaughter, Jamie, made a face. Then she said, "EEWWWWWW."

Brad laughed. "It's not so bad. Better than you think. Except when I tried it, the chocolate overwhelmed the bacon. It's okay if they keep the two in the right proportions."

The rest of us just looked at him. I gathered that

among our family there would be no takers for chocolate-covered bacon ... beyond the few bites, however many they were, already tried by Brad.

IN OTHER, WISER COUNTRIES, THE FAT ISSUE IS NOT a problem. On a trip last year to the Baltic states—Norway, Denmark, Sweden, Finland—we saw almost no overweight people. Everyone was slim, and all seemed to be walking or bicycling everywhere, at a good clip. Unlike America, nobody was eating as he walked. In fact, we've been told snacking is unheard of.

The same holds true of Buenos Aires, Argentina. During a long taxi ride recently down a narrow city boulevard I observed hundreds of people strolling along the sidewalks at above-average speeds—-and only one man among those hundreds had a moderate belly.

While we were in Buenos Aires our family was invited to an inner-courtyard dinner with an Argentinean family. Because we were guests, they lavished us with food—meat, and more meat, and then still more meat. Six or seven barbecued meat courses in all. (Most of us gave up after Number Three). But the dinner menu also included a variety of vegetables and a fresh-fruit mix for dessert.

We cannot vouch for the normal eating habits of South Americans, but judging by the look of them, they must be worlds ahead of us.

And probably taking far fewer pills.

Last Christmas my daughter-in-law, Melanie, sent us a book titled, "Eat to Live," by Joel Fuhrman, M.D. By coincidence, just as I finally picked it up to read it, the doctor himself appeared on my email with a video.

I watched the whole thing. And now I'll REALLY read his book.

I'm not sure how many seeds and weeds I can bring myself to swallow. Or how much fresh fruit I'll be able to consume. Or whether I'll be willing to buy—and then cook—the strange vegetables, like bok choy, that only I will eat … Rob having made it clear he'll eat only "normal" vegetables.

Can I, at last, finally give up ice cream? It's a question that remains to be answered.

Can I, with an improved diet, give up my daily pill for arthritis?

Hard to predict. Like all of us, whether we're Seventy or not, I'm still a work in progress.

CHAPTER TWENTY

Still Working—At Something

WE USED TO HEAR IT EVERYWHERE: *men retire and then they die* … the short way of saying that men didn't last long after they left their jobs. Forty years of work seemed to earn them only two or three Golden Years.

Remember when your mother shook her finger at you and lamented, "I don't want Dad to quit working. Men leave their jobs and think they've got nothing to live for. So they stop living." Then she'd smile and say, "Of course I never get to quit. I'm still doing his laundry and cooking his meals."

Which in those years was pretty typical.

But hey, we're all Seventy and everything has changed. Now that women go out to work nearly as often as men and retirement hits both sexes equally, do we all just "dive for the dirt" after we leave the job?

Not exactly. I've been looking around. Rob retired twelve years ago, but he's busier and happier than during his years of defending doctors and hospitals. When people ask, "What do you do with your days?" he rolls his eyes and says, "I should print up a three by five card. I wouldn't have time now to go to work," and he starts with the list ... endless yard work, managing his investments, doing cross words, reading two newspapers a day and countless magazine articles, writing essays, sending timely articles to friends, paying bills, watching the TV news, going to the theater, processing the mail pile—not to mention listening to me ... and playing Sequence with any and all of us who want to play.

And then there's my routine: Nine months a year I teach a weekly class in Novel writing and Memoirs, which entails 70 pages a week of line editing. But I also give about 50 speeches a year, edit books on the side, present yearly workshops at several writers' conferences, and am currently finishing this, my 14th book—with two more waiting to be written.

So I'm not exactly retired. I could add that my Golden Years of retirement are glimmering somewhere off in the distance—except these ARE my Golden Years.

When you love what you do, you seldom think of it as work. Now vacuuming the house or mopping the kitchen floor ... *that* would be work!

A bonus for my current lifestyle is having a husband who's not bound by tradition. "It's okay, Babe," says Rob with a smile. "For years I haven't expected you to cook dinner."

I'M NOT THE ONLY ONE PUTTING OFF RETIREMENT. Three of our current doctors are in their Seventies and none have indicated they're ready to hang up their stethoscopes. But all take frequent trips, and it's clear they don't keep the hectic schedules they once did.

One of our best friends, once a professor of surgery at a major university, bucked the trend and left his position and never looked back. Yet he's still working—at something.

"We play bridge three days a week," said his wife. "We're known as the couple who never argues. In fact, we surprise everyone that we're so congenial and courteous playing as a team."

Both were once competitive tennis players, and though they left the courts in their mid Seventies, their lives are still rich and full. Besides playing cards, doing crossword puzzles, swimming in their pool, and following professional tennis on television, the two take frequent driving trips and work in their beautiful backyard garden.

Everyone who knew him assumed this doctor would regret leaving the prestigious world of medicine.

He hasn't, not for a moment. He seems to have found the same degree of happiness he had as a high-profile surgeon. And his wife is equally enthusiastic about their retirement years. As she says, "We're creating the carefree childhood neither of us had."

AMONG OUR OTHER FRIENDS, IT'S HARD TO GENER-alize about past or present careers. Some of my female friends worked outside their homes and others didn't. Three of us were never anyone's paid employee, yet among us we raised fourteen children—which, as anyone knows, qualifies as "work." Today, for one of us, a widow, the void is filled with managing her husband's investments, but even more with committee work for groups that support the arts.

Among my "working" friends is one who was once a full-time real estate agent (now partly retired—but chairing a major charity), two who helped run their husband's professional offices (one still does), and another who has mostly retired as a literary agent—except she still represents a few long-time clients.

AS I THINK OF OUR MALE FRIENDS IN THEIR Seventies, one is still CEO of his own company, teaching on-line business courses to international students; another, a well-regarded research physicist, studies neutrinos in Japan; a third, an infectious diseases doctor who is also a violinist, is officially "retired," but continues as a clinician in a medical center—yet manages to join other musicians in giving concerts; a urologist friend who is also officially retired, recently returned to work part time in a medical center.

ROB AND I GUESS THAT WHEN THESE MEN FULLY retire they will do so in the same manner as the surgeon—sliding easily into the challenging activities they're now doing part time—as though they're just stepping into a new and equally exciting life.

AMONG THE NON-PROFIT GROUPS I BELONG TO (both are support groups for the arts), the membership is made up largely of women in an age range from fifty-five to eighty. Nobody cares how old we are as long as our checks clear—as long as we come to meetings and do the jobs we said we'd do. For years we've regularly elected presidents in their Seventies.

Whatever you once thought about Seventy being the end of everything, about people "dropping out" of life to sit on the front porch in their rocking chairs … nobody that I know personally has time or inclination to do much sitting of any kind.

Besides, it's hard to Skype your grandchildren while the chair is rocking.

All of us are looking forward, not backward. We know some very good years are still ahead. When any of us discuss age, we're apt to sum ourselves up as part of a new and different world. As one of my friends said, "Seventy is the new Fifty."

Chapter Twenty-One

Not–So–Ancient Heroes

Now that I'm trudging the last mile of this literary marathon about Americans in their Seventies, the media seems to be taking a new interest in the lives of people who were once simply called *old*. Many of them, whom I've chosen to call "heroes" have long since passed Seventy, as though that number was merely a gateway to new achievement.

Tom Erickson, the new minister of our Tustin Presbyterian Church, recently delivered a sermon in which he quoted statistics from a book called, "The Best is Yet to Be," by Henry Durbanville. The author said that 35% of the world's accomplishments were by people between the ages of 60-70. Among those 70-80, came 23% more. And yet another 6% were from seniors over 80. Totaled up, this means that 64% of the world's meaningful accomplishments were derived from people older than Sixty.

Erickson named names: Winston Churchill was

77 when he was re-elected Prime Minister of Great Britain. At 70, Susan B. Anthony became president of the Women's Suffrage Movement, a position she held until she was 77.

George C. Marshall began his Recovery Program, the Marshall Act, at age 67, and continued in that role for years.

Ronald Reagan was president until age 77.

As to the Presbyterian minister himself, an energetic man with a rich voice, he is now 78.

IT WAS ONLY A WEEK AGO THAT ROB AND I, DRIPping mustard off a Costco hot dog, asked to join a couple already at one of the store's few indoor tables. The couple, who seemed about our ages, agreed to let us take the other side of the table.

Eventually we began chatting, and learned that they lived in a nearby senior community. But the man was NOT our age, he was ninety. Yet his face was smooth and he didn't need a hearing aid or reading glasses. He'd led an interesting life. In WWII he'd been a radioman on a Navy bomber, then in later years a plumber. His wife— no, not his wife, his girlfriend—was bright-looking and trim. Now 87, she told us how for years after college she'd run the family business.

Both had been married over sixty years to other people. Now both widowed, they were well into a new, loving relationship. When they got up and left the store, they were holding hands. Rob saw her driving the two away in her Lexus. I almost expected to hear the car had a sign that said, "Just Married."

IN JULY, 2009, I FLEW TO FOREST HILLS TO WATCH my daughter play womens' doubles in the National Grass Court Tennis Championships. She was entered in the 50s category—and here I'll brag a little and report that she and her partner won the gold ball.

But the event I remember best was the singles match between two women playing in the 80s. Like everyone in the stands, I was fascinated. In broiling heat, the two walked and stumbled and lurched to return balls, and at each change of ends they both sat down on the bench to chat.

They sat so long they could have had tea between games.

Although each was playing to win, this was clearly not a life or death struggle. Even between games they paused at the net to smile and chat and hand each other balls. Anything to slow it down.

For all of us in the stands it mattered little who won. Just watching them was enough. At every opportunity we applauded vigorously, our enthusiasm centered on the fact that those two were even there, still in the game.

THE MEDIA CONTINUES ITS FASCINATION WITH AGE. Louis Zamperini, the famous Olympic runner (subject of the book *Unbroken* by Laura Hillenbrand), though frail-looking and bent over, at age 94 continues to give speeches at local churches, as I learned from a parishioner who heard him.

A whole-page article in the bulletin from the California Writers Club (San Fernando Valley), describes the team of seniors who played volleyball for the Pasadena Senior Olympics. They were talked into playing the tournament only because they were assured they'd be competing in their own age group, 70-79.

Somehow things changed. "As it turned out," Yolanda Fintor wrote, "all our games were against the 60-69 age range because there were no other teams in our age category." The games were played as round robins, with no elimination of losers. "It was a good thing," she said, "because we only won one game."

She continues, "After the games were over we were asked to line up in the lobby. We thought it was for photographs, but it was for much more than that. We received a tee shirt AND a gold medal!"

The mood going home was somber. "Does anyone else feel that this was a hollow victory?" asked Waynette.

"Yes," said Ann. "It's too bad we received recognition just for being the only ones in our age category to show up."

"But deep down," said Joyce, "we know we could have beaten another team at our level of play."

"Well, look at it this way," said Marci. "We'll proudly wear our medals over our Senior Olympic shirts." Her voice dropped to a conspiratorial whisper. "No one needs to know we won by default."

The group gave each other high-fives.

A July 4, 2012, article in the Life Wellness section of the *Orange County Register* ran a large picture of Beejay Janiga, 85, teaching one of her five weekly workout classes at the Tustin Senior Center. The article is headlined, SHE'S GOT STAMINA, and indeed it appears she does. In the picture not only is she attractive and beaming, she is clearly agile. Janiga leads her group, arms outstretched with weights clutched in each hand, marching vigorously.

Besides the five weekly workouts, which include people many years younger than Janiga herself, she also leads a dance troupe.

Another article in *The Register*, this by columnist Jane Glenn Haas, describes a KOCE/PBS and AARP presentation of the documentary, "After 90 and Loving it." The program, aired at the Huntington Beach Library, showed people in their 90s and 100s who are still living extraordinary lives.

There was Nola Ochs, a successful candidate for her masters degree at age 99. Katie Brown, aged 91, still drives to her job in a mall, where she helps prepare cinnamon rolls.

Laura Simon, age 101, is writing a second book about her life, while Harry Rakoff, 94, is still a New York City cabdriver. Les Lieber plays his saxophone every Friday in a New York club. He is 96.

With great verve, Haas describes the two oldsters whom she drove to the library event. Between them they had a century's worth of backseat driving experience. Each of them spoke up repeatedly, telling her where to turn, how to maneuver through traffic. At the end Haas said to them, "I've never had so many backseat drivers."

"So many?" one of them replied. "There are only two of us."

"WOMAN, 99, RECEIVES ACCOLADES FOR Volunteer Work." That was the headline on July 26, 2012, in the Tustin News. The article reports that Altha Gardener, after 33 years of community service, still assists with lunch service at the Tustin Area Senior Center.

AND FINALLY, ON JULY 26, 2012, THE LOS ANGELES Times published an article titled, *O'Connor Defends Chief Justice's Health Vote.*

To nobody's surprise, Sandra Day O'Connor,

appointed by President Reagan in 1981 as the Supreme Court's first woman Justice, continues to make national news.

In a story that mainly reflects O'Connor's views on the recent health care ruling by Chief Justice John G. Roberts Jr., the article notes that at age 82 O'Connor has set up an online education course to "teach middle school students about the three branches of government."

Though she retired from the Supreme Court in 2006 (to care for her husband, who died three years later), she has not retired from the world. Judge O'Connor continues to hear cases "as a visiting judge in federal district courts and courts of appeals." She has also taught at the University of Arizona and served on a commission that studied the Iraq war.

Deborah Merritt, a professor at Ohio State University's Moritz college of law, was once a clerk for O'Connor during her first Supreme Court term. Said Merritt, "I've never known anyone with her degree of energy, passion, and intelligence." When asked about the chance that O'Connor would retire, Merritt replied with a laugh. "Justice O'Connor will never retire."

WHICH IS EXACTLY HOW MANY OF US FEEL ABOUT our lives. The world is still an exciting place, and we're still having fun. As George Bernard Shaw says, "You don't stop laughing when you grow old. You grow old when you stop laughing."

We may be Seventy, but my cardiologist has it right. When I asked what patients should be doing physically at our ages, he smiled and said, "Age is just a number."

For most days it's a number we blithely ignore.

Sometimes, in our dreams, we find ourselves doing the athletic things we once did. Deep in slumber, I often ski down snowy slopes, or even oftener I'm back on the pale green court, playing tennis.

And then I wake up.

And I remember that I'm not thirty any more. And for a moment it's scary.

But I quickly reassure myself that nothing has changed, that I will go about my day pretty much as I always have—that upstairs half a book is waiting to be written ... that tonight Rob and I have been invited out for dinner with two kids and three grandkids ... that I'm poised to be as happy today as I've been for most of my life.

Because the truth is, I'm 83

About the Author

Maralys Wills has lived three distinct lives: Author of fifteen published books, teacher of college students, and mother of six children—five boys and a girl,

Educated at Stanford and UCLA, she is married to a retired trial lawyer. She currently teaches novel writing on the college level, and in 2000 was named Teacher of the Year.

Her most challenging project, a poignant memoir titled *Higher Than Eagles*, became her biggest triumph, garnering excellent reviews and five movie options.

Wills considers public speaking the dessert for

all the hard work of writing, and relishes every moment spent with a receptive audience. Contact her at Maralys@Cox.net or www.Maralys.com

Word of mouth is crucial for any author to succeed. If you enjoyed the book, please consider leaving a review on Amazon, even if it's only a line or two; it will make all the difference and is very much appreciated!

* 9 7 8 0 9 8 5 9 4 2 6 0 1 *